"There are some people," Peter said, *who believe that the Royal Orleans is the finest hotel in North America. Whether you agree or not doesn't much matter. The point is: It shows how good a hotel can be."*

From HOTEL
By Arthur Hailey

French Quarter Royalty

The Tumultuous Life and Times of the Omni Royal Orleans Hotel

John DeMers

ISBN 1-881007-00-6

Printed in the United States of America

Contents

Preface

As the fifth general manager to serve the Omni Royal Orleans, I take great pleasure in being the one to commission a book about our hotel, our history and our people. It is to them, above all, that this book must be dedicated.

Surely the idea of this book has been entertained by those who've sat at this desk before me. Indeed, many who've been our guests for only one night have suggested it. Yet the hotel business is like any other — a swift progression of urgent deadlines and even more urgent demands. As in any other business, except more so, the longterm, seemingly less essential projects get pushed to the side. It seemed time, with the beginning of my tenure at the Royal Orleans, to let this project be pushed aside no longer.

At this hotel, we are proud of our history: not only the three-plus decades since the present structure was erected but the 150-plus years our site was known as the City Exchange and the old St. Louis. From the days of flamboyant Creoles and somber slave auctions, through the Civil War and Reconstruction, through hurricanes, fires and economic despair, this site has been a place for New Orleans to gather and encounter the world. Today, as a grand hotel, we are also a place for the world to gather and encounter New Orleans.

If you live in this city, and particularly if you were born here as I was, you will recognize many names in these pages — from historical figures like "Beast" Butler to modern visionaries like Edgar Stern and Lester Kabacoff. If you are visiting us in New Orleans, and particularly if you are visiting us at the Omni Royal Orleans, you should find these pages a doorway into our Southern soul.

You will see that we recall the past a great deal more than most people do, at times revere it a tad more than we should. Yet speaking not only for our hotel but for our city, we live absolutely in the present with hope for the future. To our way of thinking, this future is all the brighter for those among us who understand and embrace the place from which we came.

Gary Froeba
General Manager

Graceful swirls of wrought iron speak volumes in the French Quarter.

Past As Prelude

*Even into the 20th century, the Creole quarter was
a world apart.*

The grand old French Opera House was the center of Creole social life.

1

The Contract

Sitting at his desk, awaiting the bankers and the two witnesses, Jacques Nicholas Bussiere DePoilly gave the contract one last, careful look. He and his brother Isadore had labored so long over each condition, each stipulation, that this time the reading had an unpleasant hollowness, like hearing an overture once too often at the French Opera House. Yet DePoilly knew better than let the moment master him. The negotiations were over. The building was about to begin.

"Les Americaines," he breathed suddenly, not without delight. He could envision them over there, on their side of Canal Street, with their allegedly grand hotel and their unsubstantiated social pretensions. The French Quarter, the real quarter, would have the last word after all.

Only a decade earlier, the issue had been a moot one. There had been no grand hotels in New Orleans, in the French or American sectors. Visitors had stayed in small rooming houses like Tremoulet's. A pair of larger establishments did exist, the Hotel d'Orleans and the Hotel d'Estrangers; but these were hardly grand in the manner the Quarter's Europeans knew by experience or at least by reputation.

The St. Charles had changed all that the year before, rising up on the American side as a symbol of what its backers saw as the city's future. No more dreary Creole langor, countless numbing libations and insatiable quadroon mistresses. The Americans were building a new city devoted to progress - to future-thinking commerce conducted in English - and the St. Charles was its hub. Its tall dome was often compared to the masterpiece atop St. Paul's Cathedral in London.

What was it DePoilly had read only recently? Oh yes... "In St. Petersburg, you would think it a palace. In Boston you would christen it a college. In London it would marvelously remind you of an exchange. In New Orleans it is all three."

Such ecstatic paeans sickened the heart of any true Creole, for they bolstered the threat that the Americans just might be right. They might be right about the city, right about the future, right about their own growing numbers and financial might. Yet they were not right, DePoilly insisted. They were wrong, and the project facing him amidst the agreements and drawings would prove them wrong forever.

The architect smiled, glancing about among the words he had written in a letter attached to the contract. "The desire to have myself known as a contractor," he had scripted in French, "and to affix my signature toward the accomplishment of an edifice for which I have an affectionate feeling due to a habit I have contracted by working at it...."

DePoilly's smile broadened. A habit he had contracted indeed! The contract promised him a $220,000 habit, due in five equal payments. "I believe," he had concluded, "I can promise work of a careful and solid nature, and especially shall I strive to deliver the buildings within the prescribed time."

The time! It was almost time for the bankers and the two witnesses. Growing serious, DePoilly flipped through to the final page, passing over hundreds of conditions that for months had been his obsession... "shall be measured in accordance with the rules of geometry without regard for any contrary practices... the handrail of the stairway of the large hall shall be made a la francaise with decorated screat rings and platbands set in bars... the floorings shall be of cypress of the first grade...." There, on the contract's last page, was the promised completion date - May 1, 1838.

They could have the St. Charles with its dome, he thought. Who needed London or Boston or St. Petersburg in New Orleans anyway? What this city needed was a Creole palace, a place for aristocrats to meet and do business, to eat and drink and make love, to buy slaves and sell plots of land on the banks of the Mississippi. The city needed a hotel worthy of - itself!

DePoilly was convinced he would build such a hotel, a royal presence in the heart of the French Quarter, a beacon telling all the world that New Orleans was a world apart. Most of all, it would be a beacon to the one group DePoilly hoped most fervently would look on in dismay.

"Les Americaines," he said, hearing the knock at his office door. This time the word was almost a snarl.

The old slave auction block.

2

City Exchange

The hotels that would be the legacy of the contract DePoilly signed on February 23, 1838, would operate under a series of names - the St. Louis, the Hotel Royal and finally the Omni Royal Orleans. They would suffer fires and hurricanes, political upheaval and fiscal nightmare. Yet they would remain, in the truest sense, precisely what DePoilly and the Company of Amelioration called their original creation: the City Exchange. For business or the extremes of pleasure, from slave auctions to corporate takeovers, the grand hotel on St. Louis Street between Royal and Chartres would be the place that the old Creole city took on the world and the future.

Though in time the struggle between Creoles and Americans would subside - eventually it would have to, in a city increasingly American - the long memory of its combatants would remind New Orleanians forever they were different from the rest. Their roots were different, and their spirits were different. Their formation lay, as DePoilly had expressed so well in the details of his hotel, not in the restless ambitions of the New World but in the demanding standards of the Old.

Unlike most of the United States, which took on the flavor (such as it was) of its British overlords, New Orleans grew from the tangle of brilliance and corruption that was France at its most grandiose. The Quarter that rose up along the Mississippi River was, like the railings of the main staircase in DePoilly's hotel, distinctly "a la francaise."

It was a French explorer exotically named Rene Robert Cavalier, Sieur de La Salle, who set out from Canada to find the mouth of the river. He followed the Mississippi all the way to the Gulf of Mexico and its huge delta of swamps, humidity and disease. Noting that in one way or the other, nearly all of this undiscovered territory drained into the river that drained into the Gulf of Mexico, La Salle claimed it all for France. In honor of the Sun King, Louis XIV, he christened this land Louisiane.

From the moment exploration and settlement got under way, both had an unmistakable French flair. More ambitious men threw their web of names into the history books, led off by Pierre le Moyne, Sieur d'Iberville, and his younger brother Jean-Baptiste le Moyne, Sieur de Bienville. These two established French colonies in Ocean Springs on the Gulf coast, then in Mobile, Natchez and Natchitoches. In 1718, Bienville picked out one additional site on the banks of the Mississippi and named it after the regent of the Sun King's great grandson, Philippe, duc d'Orleans. La Nouvelle Orleans the site would be. The new Orleans.

From quite early in their history, the French settlers of New Orleans made it no secret they considered the city theirs. As descendants of these immigrants came to be called Creoles, they donned with all seriousness the air of running the place that newcomers sought to wrestle away only at their peril. When New Orleans was ceded to Spain in 1762, first by the Treaty of Fountainbleau and finally by the Treaty of Paris, the city rebelled. It had taken four years for word of

Spanish rule to reach New Orleans, so its inhabitants decided an almost equal period of violence was a fair exchange. Ever blessed with a sense of pragmatism, however, the French Creoles decided they could live with Spain when 24 warships and 2,000 troops pulled up at their docks. The Spanish had some culture, after all. And they were even more corrupt than the French, so the locals opted to learn from the masters as much as they could.

It was Napoleon Bonaparte, that beacon of Frenchness, who talked Spain into giving Louisiana back - but only so he could sell it to the young, rough-talking, woefully backwoods Americans. It was a blow from which the Creoles never quite recovered. With the payment of $15 million at the Cabildo overlooking what is now Jackson Square, the entire Louisiana Territory became property of the United States. Nine years later, in 1812, Louisiana was admitted into the Union.

Creole ladies and gentlemen at the French Opera House.

The stage was set, from this moment on, for the battle that New Orleans' two grand hotels evoked so well. Americans poured down the river on anything that would float, bent on making their fortunes in New Orleans. With their fortunes or at least livelihoods suddenly in jeopardy, the Creoles turned away in anger.

Virtually forbidden to venture into the city's French Quarter, the Americans began erecting impressive homes on the far side of what was intended to be a drainage canal. Fights between Creoles and Americans were commonplace, with the strip of land separating the two groups becoming known as the "neutral ground." At least some of these disputes, begun in a bar or coffeehouse, ended on a tombstone inscribed "Mort sur le champ d'honneur." The wide boulevard separated by a median later was named for the canal that never was: Canal Street.

As late as the day DePoilly signed his contract, the Creoles of New Orleans continued to educate their children in France, to conduct all affairs in French and indeed to center their lives around their thoroughly French families and their equally French culture center, the French Opera House. There was great pride and self-satisfaction in this stance, but a kind of guaranteed obsolesence as well. Reject the thought as much as they might, the French aristocracy doomed itself to affronts like the St. Charles Hotel simply by refusing to move ahead. It was neither the first nor the last such refusal in the history of New Orleans.

❈ ❈ ❈

By the early 1800s, the Creoles of New Orleans had established themselves as "cafe society" in the most literal sense possible. They loved their cafes, from the Cafe des Ameliorations frequented by the militantly unreconstructed to the Cafe des Emigres favored by French planters who had fled the bloody slave uprising in Santo Domingo. Yet the single most famous of all cafes stood at the site on which DePoilly would build his grand hotel.

La Bourse de Maspero, or Maspero's Exchange, is described as a two-story wooden building that had its main entrance on Chartres Street but stretched for 90 feet along St. Louis. The city's merchants and brokers embraced Pierre Maspero's cafe and coffeehouse, conducting their business over innumerable cups of coffee and considerably more incendiary beverages. The cafe and its kitchens took up the entire ground floor of Maspero's Exchange, with a bar running the main room's entire length. The floor was of sand, with small tables squeezed into every possible space. The journalists of New Orleans held down a special corner in which several tables had been pushed together. Editors and reporters met for lunch here each day, turning the news of the day tirelessly before their eyes.

Though many cafes still claim the honor, it is possible that Gen. Andrew Jackson planned 1815's Battle of New Orleans here. We do know Jackson held several meetings at the Exchange, going over strategy with his officers in a room on the second floor. That's considerably more evidence than most of the other claimants can mount - particularly the several that did not even exist in 1815.

Pierre Maspero himself ran the cafe into the era that DePoilly was drawing up his plans. In 1838, however, it was taken over by high-roller James Hewlett, who logically enough changed its name to Hewlett's Exchange. The new owner changed a good deal more than Maspero's name, however. He covered the sand floor with cypress and installed a new bar proclaimed the finest in all New Orleans. After enlarging the kitchen and restaurant facilities, he constructed an auction area in which stocks, real estate and other properties were sold daily from noon until three. Saturdays were set aside for the sale of slaves, considered an essential part of a man's portfolio until the Civil War.

Upstairs at the Exchange, the fancy of both Hewlett and

his patrons turned to gaming. Every form of gambling was available, as were tables devoted to the exotic game called billiards. In an adjacent building, Hewlett added yet another popular sport of his day, cockfighting. In one of his more unusual moves, he bankrolled an Englishman who opened a curiosity on St. Louis right behind the Exchange: a bar that sold only beer.

DePoilly's plans, indeed DePoilly's vision, called for an enormous building that would replace the Exchange and cover the entire block formed by Royal, Toulouse, Chartres and St. Louis Streets. It would, in fact, reproduce the majesty of the Rue de Rivoli in Paris. Work began shortly after the contract was signed. A financial crisis struck shortly thereafter, however, and everyone involved was forced to scale down the design. By the time the Exchange opened its doors during the summer of 1938, it occupied only the side of the square fronting on St. Louis St.

All the same, breathless accounts of the day make it clear the Creoles were impressed. The main entrance on St. Louis opened into a vestibule 127 feet wide and 40 feet deep. And the bar was memorialized by one British visitor as "not quite as large as the reading room of the British Museum." There were lush ballrooms on the second floor, with entrances on both Royal and St. Louis streets. One of these featured a ceiling painted by Domenico Canova that drew praise for "beauty unsurpassed in America." On the top two floors, there were enough rooms to accommodate 600 guests.

Yet most excitement focused on the hotel's Rotunda, a circular space with a high-domed ceiling in the very center of the building. This replaced the now-levelled Hewlett's Exchange as the city's principal auction mart.

One visitor of the period described the scene this way: "Each auctioneer was endeavoring to drown out every voice but his own... One was selling pictures and dwelling on their merits; another was disposing of ground-lots of embryo cities... and another was disposing of slaves. These consisted of an unhappy negro family, who were all exposed to the hammer at the same time. Their good qualities were enumerated in English and in French, and their persons were carefully examined by intending purchasers, among whom they were ultimately disposed of, chiefly to Creole buyers; the husband at 750 dollars, the wife at 550, and the children at 220 each."

In this same rotunda, English writer John Galsworthy stood 72 years later, surrounded by what few memories had survived war, conflagration and hurricane. An old woman lighted newspapers to show him the once-lively slave block. "Yes suh," she told Galsworthy. "Here they all came - 'twas the finest hotel - before the war-time; old Southern families - buyin' and sellin' their property... And here were the bells to all the rooms. Broken, you see - all broken!"

Who better to manage the Exchange than Pierre Maspero himself, assisted in the bar and restaurant by a Spaniard named Alvarez. Of course, Alvarez is not terribly well-known; yet two of the innovations attributed to him are dramatically written into the culinary history of New Orleans. In a world that remembers Escoffier at the Ritz and Oscar at the Waldorf, perhaps Alvarez at the Exchange should be recalled more often.

It is hard to imagine anyone "inventing" gumbo, for the immeasurably wonderful Creole soup or stew seems woven of the very soul of New Orleans. Its name derives from the West African word for okra, "gombo," the seeds of which were brought by slaves to help them cling to the flavors of home. Yet someone must have been the first to use these strange-looking pods to thicken a powerfully flavored fish soup, taking it in one stroke from the thinly brothed bouillabaisse of Marseilles to the rich and glorious gumbo of New Orleans. According to more legends than can be dismissed offhand, that someone was Alvarez.

Though less significant culinarily, the second innovation introduced at the City Exchange was at least as intriguing. It was here that Alvarez (perhaps remembering the tapas of

Etching of the original Exchange Hotel.

Spain) set out the first free lunch ever served in New Orleans - and perhaps in America as well. The menu consisted of soup, a piece of beef or ham with potatoes, meat pie and oyster patties. At the start, these dishes were handed to the customer with whatever drink he had ordered. Later, the food was simply displayed on a counter where anyone could enjoy as much as he chose.

The idea proved so popular that it soon was picked up by all the first-class bars in New Orleans. Within a few years, bars all over the country were putting out free feasts that compared to some of the best meals in their neighborhoods.

Alvarez must have been successful with these and other creative touches, for early in 1840 he replaced Pierre Maspero as manager of the Exchange. The bar and restaurant were placed in the hands of one Joseph Santini, who is remembered as the inventor of two drinks beloved in their day - the Crusta and Santini's Pousse-Cafe. These were such widely copied potables they were featured in a bartender's bible published early in this century, The Bon Vivant's Companion, or How to Mix Drinks.

❋ ❋ ❋

In early 1841, the City Exchange - or the St. Louis, as the Creoles had taken to calling it in defiance of the Americans - was destroyed by the first of its fires. Using DePoilly's original plans, however, the owners quickly rebuilt and entered upon the hotel's golden age. Alvarez was replaced as manager by yet another familiar face, none other than James Hewlett. It was during Hewlett's reign that the St. Louis became the glittering center of a social scene impossible to replicate today.

Though the nearby Orleans Ballroom had long held the favor of Creole gentlemen, particularly for its infamous "quadroon balls" of coffee-colored mistresses-to-be; the St. Louis throughout the 1840s and 1850s was the scene of French New Orleans' most lavish banquets and masquerades. Hewlett introduced a series of subscription balls that became the envy of society in New York, Boston and Newport. The most notable of these was given during the winter of 1842-43 in honor of Henry Clay, complete with music by the French Opera House orchestra. As 600 subscribers paid $100 each, the ball and supper rang in at a then-astronomical $60,000.

Hewlett also managed to establish his hotel as the heartbeat of a celebration that enthralled the city each winter season. Certainly, many of the Creoles carried memories of Carnival in Nice or Venice. And certainly, these memories first took form in the New World when a group called the Cowbellions paraded in Mobile. Yet with a bold assist from Hewlett and his grand hotel, the carnival known as Mardi Gras became one of the most unbelievable parties on the face of the earth. The first procession with decorated floats hit the streets in 1837. But until formation of the Mystick Krewe of

Comus in 1857, the primary observance of Mardi Gras was not on the streets at all. It was in the lush ballrooms of the St. Louis Hotel.

Henry Clay is remembered as the Great Compromiser, for his tireless efforts at heading off a split between North and South over slavery. His efforts paid off in Missouri in 1820, in South Carolina in 1833, in New Mexico, Utah and California in 1850. Yet even as he basked in the St. Louis' glory, he must have sensed that time was running out. Both sides were becoming impatient, almost longing for the day that bloodshed would silence the debate. The hotel that lavished its attentions on the Great Compromiser would soon find itself at the center of New Orleans' suffering. The hotel that played host to society's elite would soon play host to war, occupation and the cruelest Reconstruction.

*Travelers from all corners of the globe admired the
rotunda of the St. Louis Hotel.*

3

Battle Zone

*I*t was not American history's "shot heard round the world," for that had been fired at Concord years earlier. But the first shot fired at Ft. Sumter was most assuredly heard by both Creoles and Americans in New Orleans. The city's importance to both sides in the Civil War was understood intuitively by the citizenry: a near-guarantee that one of the conflict's bloodiest battles would be fought in their very streets. That fact that this battle was never fought is a tribute to the bravery, or to the cowardice, or to the sheer pragmatism of the city's leadership. Perhaps, as has so often been the case in New Orleans, it is a blend of all three.

All through the spring of 1862, Brigadier General Benjamin Buisson worked to keep his faith in his city's ability to defend itself, to retain hope by poring over the booklet titled "Instruction pour le Service de la Batterie de Garde d'Orleans." But on April 24th, this veteran French fighting man was awakened by the sound he had most feared, the pealing of twelve fire bells fours times over. The federal fleet under

29

Capt. Farragut had slipped past Forts Jackson and St. Philip. Now, nothing but Buisson's battery of men too old or ill for other fronts stood between the Yankees and New Orleans.

The scene surrounding the Hotel St. Louis was a nightmare: mud streets jammed with carts and wagons, each loaded with a Creole family's quickly assembled possessions. Small lynch mobs pushed their way through the hysteria, seeking to string up anyone suspected of being a Union sympathizer. When darkness fell, the entire spectacle was lit by eerie quivering light from fires along the river. Steamboat wood, bales of cotton and even whole vessels had been ignited to keep them out of Northern hands. That seemingly timeless underclass of looters responded to the call, making off with everything from molasses to baby carriages.

Buisson remembered that in all his years fighting beside Napoleon, he had seen many cities sacked. But as he put it later, this was the first he had seen sacked by its own inhabitants.

Finally, Farragut's 13 ships sailed round Slaughter House Point and anchored less than one hundred yards off the levee of New Orleans. Its masts were clearly visible from the upper floors of the St. Louis. A Union officer fought his way through the crowd of locals to find Mayor John T. Monroe and his advisor Pierre Soule. Standing at the heart of a city at least as endangered by its own hysterical excess as by any Yankee guns, the officer watched in amazement as his demand for surrender launched a dizzying game of diplomatic chess.

Day followed day as Soule concocted one ruse after another, one legal technicality after another to prevent the city from giving up its own ghost. That flag must be struck? Oh no, monsieur, that flag is not under this jurisdiction but under another, and the only person who can authorize that is not here! Nowhere else could Confederate stubbornness find such an ally in Creole posturing. "We will stand your bombardment," Soule wrote in the name of the mayor, "unarmed and undefended as we are. The civilized world will condemn to indelible infamy the heart that will conceive the deed and the hand that will dare to consummate it."

As it turned out, the Creoles kept on finding loopholes until the Yankees themselves lowered the Confederate flags all around the city. Soule's threat of "indelible infamy" was destined to fall not upon the one who conquered New Orleans but on the one who arrived to oversee its occupation.

It must have been a satisfaction to Creoles who loved the St. Louis that General Benjamin F. Butler chose as his headquarters the St. Charles Hotel. Nothing could have expressed better the feverish fact that the St. Charles was not truly French - that its very existence was in some way an act of treason. As the St. Louis embarked on its wartime career as a U.S. military hospital, it could gloat that its American counterpart was the official home address of the "Beast."

It seemed to be Butler's commission, and most assuredly his delight, to break the spirit of New Orleans wherever it raised its unsurrendering head. He offered freedom to any slave who informed upon his master, thus threatening many heads of Creole households with prison. Intriguingly, Butler met his match among Creole women, who took pride in

Later view of the St. Louis.

teaching their children to spit on passing Yankee soldiers and who giggled pointedly at any Yankee funeral. After some of these tough ladies turned their backs on Butler on the street, he remarked, "Those women evidently know which end of them looks best." And in the infamous General Order No. 28, he held that any woman showing contempt for his troops "shall be regarded and held liable to be treated as a woman of the town plying her avocation."

With the hindsight of history, it is clear that Beast Butler was not without his good works. He did feed the poor - albeit with money he extracted from local commerce - and he did lift the city to a level of cleanliness it had never known. "Butler," observed one Confederate wit, "was the best scavenger New Orleans ever had." Medical facilities such as the St. Louis were more sanitary than anything the city had known before the war, and cleaner than many the city would know for years afterward. But the fact remains that Butler's time in the city distilled in one hated human form all the despair, disgrace and resentment the occupied city could mount in its defense.

✿ ✿ ✿

If the hotel did its duty during the years of bloodshed and stubbornly held onto its pride during occupation, all such memories faded during Reconstruction. Refocusing itself to a life of serving guests, the hotel struggled through the immediate postwar period with little enthusiasm and even less working capital. Deterioration begun during the Civil War continued under a quick succession of overseers, until in 1874 the National Building Association sold the property to the state of Louisiana for $235,000. The transaction propelled the St. Louis into the darkest and most violent period in its history.

In a series of confrontations that pitted defeated South against victorious North and, yes, black against white, the St.

Tariff from the St. Louis, from March 17, 1867.

Louis didn't just have a view of the battlefield. On several key occasions between 1874 and 1877, as the seat of Louisiana's government, it became the battlefield.

Today, we are struck by the absence of any "good side" in Reconstruction, despite the existence of individual heroism on both sides. The installation of puppet governments goes against the declared values of the United States. Yet those in New Orleans who fought to expel "carpetbaggers" clung to a belief that embraced slavery as a fact of life and denigrated blacks with a blindness that cannot now be tolerated. Thus, the battlelines of Reconstruction in New Orleans were drawn - running right through the St. Louis Hotel.

As has been observed at other periods in Louisiana's political history, one must dig into the warring sects of Lebanon to find anything quite so tangled. At some points during Reconstruction, there were actually two governments at work in the state, both claiming the right to rule from separate buildings in New Orleans.

Many books detail the endless wrangling that went on within the St. Louis, surrounded by walls that only a few years earlier had witnessed Creoles dancing to the strains of the French Opera House orchestra. Yet the hotel found an additional place in history during two explosions of hate that helped bring Louisiana's Reconstruction to its end: the White League's "Battle of Liberty Place" in 1874 and its siege of the Statehouse in 1877.

In general, New Orleanians have consigned Liberty Place and the events of September 14, 1874, to the shadows of history, so foreign do they seem to the city's values today. In the 1980s, in fact, Mayor Dutch Morial removed the last physical reminder of this battle, an obelisk standing at the site on Canal Street as memorial to White League "martyrs."

These 16 men died for a cause they saw as both holy and profound, one their leaders portrayed in terms of God-given rights to self-rule, of abuses committed by unscrupulous outsiders preserved in authority by illegal force. Yet it was a cause most assuredly fed by a vein of racism at least as deep as its inevitable vein of self-interest. Thus, when we read of the 15-minute battle that liberated the foot of Canal Street from its Metropolitan Police oppressors, we find it impossible to cheer the victors or mourn the defeated.

The day after this battle, victorious White Leaguers marched on the Statehouse, defended by a militia variously described as 450 to 3,000 strong. A bloodbath seemed likely, considering the zeal of the White League and the fortress-strength of DePouilly's building. Yet when the troops reached the St. Louis, all they saw was a white flag of surrender. During the night, the entire defense force had deserted. A drawing preserved from Frank Leslie's Illustrated Newspaper shows the scene, looking on from Chartres Street as the large, cheering crowd takes possession of the Statehouse without a shot being fired.

Despite positive reaction from the national media ("The frightful mismanagement of affairs in Louisiana under the present administration has wrought out its logical result," wrote the *New York Tribune*), the victory was shortlived. Within days of Liberty Place, President Ulysses S. Grant launched a new series of edicts enforced with fresh troops and three fresh warships. Grant's actions kept the White League conflict seething right into the notorious national and state elections of 1876.

Suffice it to say that Rutherford B. Hayes was awarded the White House by a single electoral vote, 185 to 184. And suffice it to say that on January 8, 1877, there were two inaugurations in New Orleans - Gov. Stephen B. Packard at the St. Louis and Gov. Francis T. Nicholls at Lafayette Square. Louisiana again had two warring governments, with the White League squarely behind Nicholls and armed for a fight.

"Fort Packard" - that's what the locals called the State-house during the four-month siege mounted by 3,000 White Leaguers. "Let no one be hurt, however obnoxious he may be," declared Gov. Nicholls, "and let the people of the whole country see that we are law-abiding, just and moderate."

Those same qualities, apparently, did not prevent Nicholls from negotiating a deal that gave Hayes Louisiana's disputed vote and the presidency - or from collecting his part of the bargain on April 24, 1877. On that day, the new man in the White House ordered all federal troops out of New Orleans. Without their presence, Packard immediately surrendered the Statehouse. In the same soaring rotunda that had witnessed slave auctions and Civil War casualties, Louisiana's bloody Reconstruction came to an end.

Peeling paint made the rotunda a sad sight indeed.

4

An Eerie Silence

For the remaining 40 years of its life as the St. Louis, the fondly remembered haunt of Creole ladies and gentlemen was reduced to cycles of hope and despair. As is so often the case in business, fond memories proved not nearly enough.

There were moments of pride and wishful thinking, of course - each time a notice ran in the local press that the old hotel was trying again. One announcement, for instance, crowed that one Charles L. Gumvel would be in charge, noting that he "had for many years been a great favorite of the patrons of the establishment." The notice, published in the *Delta* newspaper, went on in some detail: "The price of the board is fixed at a very moderate rate - $2 per day and $2.50, and when we consider in connection with this fact that the table of the St. Louis has always been sans reproche, and is not likely to lose any of its reputation, under the supervision of Mr. Gumvel, it must be admitted that the terms are as reasonable as even the most economical could expect."

In this announcement, even the "most economical" patrons were promised things that only the elite had once enjoyed: sleeping apartments well located for both sunlight and ventilation, numberless comforts for families, and a "corps of servants perfectly drilled in all their duties."

In 1884, two years after the state capitol had been transferred from New Orleans to Baton Rouge, the government leased the building to a man named R.J. Rivers in hopes he could make a go of it. Despite the handwriting on the wall, Rivers did what he could to remodel the structure, operating it with little success for eight years before giving up. He ran his business as the Hotel Royal, perhaps in hopes of leaving behind memories of a Yankee military hospital and a carpetbag Statehouse. Yet the memories no more went away than the name "St. Louis Hotel" wrought on the iron railings of the veranda.

There was another force that helped write the sad final chapter for the St. Louis, a force that Creoles of the French Quarter had feared from the start. It was called "change." People simply didn't go where they used to go, didn't do what they used to do. Other hotels were springing up on both sides of Canal Street, making off with revenue from renting rooms. And as for food and wine - these were being served more and more in something the Quarter's tangle of rooming houses had never forseen: restaurants!

Not only did the St. Charles continue to prosper (despite its association with Beast Butler), but more modest properties came into a period of success. In the American sector, the Verandah and the City Hotel kept up brisk business for a time, as did another called the Denechaud. As the new century approached, a new attitude approached with it. The Grunewald opened on Baronne Street, beginning a long saga that would see it become the Roosevelt and finally the Fairmont. Even in the French Quarter, things were changing - despite the conviction of many the neighborhood would remain a slum. The Monteleone, though considerably smaller than the property known by that name today, provided at least a slim beacon of hope.

Presumably because the start-up capital was less than for a hotel, restaurants opened at a fever pitch during the final years of the 19th century. Each provided another excuse for New Orleanians not to dine at the St. Louis.

Some of these places are now but memories. Moreau's on Canal Street was reputed to be the best, while Fabacher's on Royal was almost certainly the largest - serving up to 2,000 meals each day, 5,000 on Mardi Gras. Begue's was a Creole landmark near the French Market, famed for its gargantuan breakfasts of seafoods, meats and wine that could last up to four hours. The oldest surviving restaurant shares its fate, to some degree, with the St. Louis, opening as a small boarding house in 1840 directly across from the hotel. Two moves and much needed expansion later, the boarding house founded by Antoine Alciatore of Marseilles is world-famous as Antoine's.

As can be readily understood, all these new hotels and new restaurants were precisely what the old Creoles had feared, precisely what they had sensed in the wind as they glared at the splendor of the St. Charles and knew that they needed a hotel like that. They had had a hotel like that, if anything a hotel grander still. Yet war and reconstruction had piece by piece taken it away from them, like a dishonest waiter stealing one silver knife or fork at a time.

R.J. Rivers eventually turned the St. Louis back to the state, which for its part sold the real estate toward the close of the century. The doors were shut, after interested parties made off with whatever they could take. No other tenant was ever found.

❖ ❖ ❖

Intriguingly, just as there was no money to rescue the St. Louis ruins from decay, for years there was no money to tear them down. It remained an abandoned fortress in the center of French Quarter life - being allowed to welcome guests again only when some tourist paid 25 cents for a tour. Among the tourists who paid for a look were English novelist John Galsworthy and his wife Ada, who found themselves stepping through the ruins on a warm March day in 1912. They shook their heads repeatedly, as Galsworthy would record in an essay, over the "mildew and dirt, the dark denuded dankness of that old hotel, rotting with damp and time."

In his collection titled "The Inn of Tranquility," Galsworthy described his haunted walk-through, into guest rooms of dark peeling wallpaper, along crumbling galleries bequeathed to pigeons, even beneath the painted faces of the great St. Louis rotunda itself.

The St. Louis, after it had been abandoned.

"The heavy dampness ran down the stained walls and trickled into pools on the crumbling black and white marble flooring on which they stood," wrote Galsworthy. "And down in the halls there came to us wandering - strangest thing that ever strayed through deserted grandeur - a brown, broken horse, lean, with a sore flank and a head of trendous age. It stopped and gazed at us, as though we might be going to give it things to eat, then passed on, stumbling over the ruined marbles. For a moment we had thought him a ghost - one of the many. But he was not, since his hoofs sounded. The scrambling clatter of them died out into silence...."

Ada Galsworthy added a postscript to her husband's published essay, writing of the visit to a friend. "New Orleans is half-and-halfer," she wrote, "a most queer place, and we are glad to have been there." Specifically, she said of the St. Louis in ruins: "For gruesome unfaked melancholy, I've never seen anything like it."

This gruesome melancholy was not to linger much longer. Only two years after the Galsworthys' visit, during hysteria over bubonic plague, the structure was condemned as a breeding ground for rats and other infected vermin. Yet even before a demolition team could be formed, the great hurricane of 1915 did most of its work. All that remained when the wind stopped howling was rubble to be carted off.

The Legend Lives Again

This was how the site looked when Edgar Stern started imagining a grand hotel here.

A young Lester Labacoff relaxes at Longue Vue with Edith Stern, Rosa Healey Hester and Edgar Stern.

5

Birth Of A Notion

emories of the St. Louis lingered on among those with long memories, particularly among French Quarter habitues who met over drinks to bemoan the passage of time. With precisely that passage, these included fewer and fewer who considered themselves Creoles or even descendants thereof. Mostly, such sessions were conducted by an odd assortment of artists, shopkeepers and amateur historians who believed in honoring the memory of the increasingly ramshackle Quarter they knew as their neighborhood.

As for the site itself, few paused during their strolls along Royal Street or crossing to Chartres via St. Louis to ponder the glories that had once existed there. No monuments or plaques stood ready to remind, so that only those who remembered on their own - who had seen an old photo, or whose parents or grandparents had spun a colorful tale - only those bothered to gaze in through the thick tropical foliage to the emptiness that had once been full. For years there was a lumberyard on the property, saying much about what had happened to its value as real estate. Into the 1950s, there was a small praline shop fronting the street, forcing some to give into a sweet tooth now and again, even if they carried no memory at all.

No one remembers wishing a hotel would reappear where the old St. Louis had stood, and certainly no one remembers thinking seriously about building one. There had been no new hotel constructed in New Orleans in decades, with the Roosevelt and the St. Charles dominating the scene on the far side of Canal Street. Their success, and the parade of statesmen, movie stars and financiers who passed through their doors, seemed to prove that the Americans had been right about New Orleans. They had always seen the Quarter as a slum, and over the decades of the 20th century it had learned to live down to their expectations.

The story of how such a hotel was envisioned again is, in many ways, the story of how the French Quarter learned to live again. It is the story of how a "slum" - for such it was almost universally called into the second half of this century - ceased gazing at its past and started reaching for its future. It is the story of how the Quarter, with those who understood and believed in it, stopped counting its weaknesses and discovered that its blessings were nearly numberless.

It's hard to say whether any of this would have happened without a young Wall Street lawyer and an aging tycoon-philanthropist who decided he wanted to live a little longer. "If I helped him do that," Lester Kabacoff observes today, "I did a very wonderful thing, because Mr. Stern was the most wonderful man I ever knew."

❖ ❖ ❖

Edgar Stern, along with his wife Edith, is remembered today as one of the greatest philanthropists New Orleans had ever known. Schools, museums, auditoriums, housing developments for the poor and even the financially hounded New

Orleans Symphony owed whatever existence they had to the Sterns. Even their home, known as Longue Vue and valued at $8 million, was donated to a foundation by Edith Stern at the time of her death. A codicil to Edgar Stern's will expressed the couple's philosophy quite well: "In our family tradition, we have always preferred making gifts during life rather than waiting until the end of our lives to act." Despite their financial generosity, neither Edgar nor Edith Stern was primarily a "check writer." Both spent their lives creating new ideas and inspiring new values for the people of the city.

Of course, all this did carry a pricetag and did demand substantial wealth. After his education at Tulane and Harvard, Stern entered the family cotton business, Lehman, Stern and Co. As longtime treasurer of the firm, he also served for a time as president of the New Orleans Cotton Exchange, while his list of professional and civic achievements seems without end. One of his wisest strokes proved to be marrying Edith Rosenwald, daughter of Julius Rosenwald of Chicago, former head of the Sears Corporation. Together, their commitment and generosity made them models to all who might aspire to do good in the world, Edgar until his death in 1959, Edith until hers in 1980.

The first time Lester Kabacoff met Edgar Stern, he was neither a Wall Street lawyer nor what he became later, a developer-visionary first of the French Quarter and then of New Orleans' long-tawdry riverfront. Kabacoff was a World War II serviceman living with the Sterns. After the War, Stern invited Kabacoff to return from New York and his promising law career to serve as his executive assistant. And one of the first projects he was asked to assist in was the fascinating if not very hopeful notion of building a hotel in the French Quarter.

The idea, Stern said, had been put forward by none other than Lyle Aschaffenburg - the legendary hotelier who had created the Pontchartrain on St. Charles Avenue. The idea was to acquire the site of the St. Louis and take that legendary property as a model for something that would work in the modern age. Early on, it was common to speak of this proposal as a "restoration" of the St. Louis, despite the fact there was virtually nothing to restore. When the lumberyard decided to move out in 1948, Stern and his son Edgar Jr. moved in, establishing WDSU-TV opening upon Royal Street's graceful Broulatour Courtyard and sending forth Kabacoff to find a hotel deal.

As Stern's envoy recalls, the search for investment and even encouragement was long and mostly depressing. Original interest from a committee headed up by Aschaffenburg faded early on, while Conrad Hilton himself was uninterested after touring the site with Kabacoff. The head of Sheraton came down to look without results, agreeing with Hilton and others that perhaps a thoroughly modern hotel might have some future but nothing with expensive links to the past grandeur. Yet the Sterns were adamant. "They believed," recalls Kabacoff, "that only a fine luxury hotel, constructed according to traditional French Quarter architecture, should be built on this historic spot."

None of the major hotel companies who took the Kaba- coff Tour wanted to put money into the property envisioned by the Royal St. Louis Co., though several offered to come in afterward and manage it for a fee and a percentage of the profits. The Sterns initially resisted a major investment as well, based on the traditional wisdom that hotels offered high risk and limited return. "Kabby," they said to their young representative, "you go do it."

It took several years of hope and disappointment, but "do it" Kabacoff did. When there was interest in another city, Kabacoff flew there to check it it. When someone wished to meet in New Orleans, Kabacoff met with him too, as many times as it took. Contact led to contact led to contact, with the road finally leading to Equitable Life Insurance in New York, which after hearing of the hotel in detail agreed to take on a mortgage.

There remained $1.5 million to raise to get the project moving, and neither the Sterns nor their many contacts in the financial community were interested in even a piece of it. "Mr. Stern," remembered Kabacoff, "could have put up the money and owned the entire equity. But he grew up in a generation for whom hotels were not good business. Virtually every hotel in the country went bankrupt during the Great Depression." Yet Kabacoff kept after the necessary funds, making his pitches over dinners in all the Creole palaces and all the way to the hole on golf courses. It was at precisely such a hole, after shooting a birdie on the 18th at New Orleans Country Club, that Darwin Fenner of Merrill Lynch became the hotel's first investor, to the tune of $50,000. Richard W. Freeman of A.B. Freeman followed suit, taking $100,000.

"Kabby," said Edgar Stern, finally, "you've built this hotel. How much do you want me to take?" The figure settled on was $200,000, an amount matched shortly thereafter by William G. Helis Jr. and increased by $75,000 from Gen. Kemper Williams (whose generosity later created the Historic New Orleans Collection across Royal Street from the Royal Orleans). It's a safe statement that all $1.5 million was raised against the investors' better judgment. It's a safer statement that when it came time to write the checks, they trusted Kabacoff even more.

❖ ❖ ❖

The search for a company to manage the proposed hotel reaped an unexpected benefit, especially since several big-name operations had expressed interest in a contract as long as it required no cash outlay. Finding a company, Kabacoff knew, would be easy. Finding the right company would be harder. And finding a company willing to invest just might prove impossible. "There I was," recalls Kabacoff somewhat wryly, "all alone with this hotel."

Trips to the Atlantic resort of Sea Island, Ga., and also to the landmark Peabody Hotel in Memphis both proved fruitless. One day a call came through from Kabacoff's old firm in New York. There was a man worth meeting, said the partner, and he was even coming to New Orleans to attend a convention. A meeting was arranged. The man's name was Roger Sonnabend. His company was Hotel Corporation of America, which later changed its name to Sonesta.

"With our wives, Sonnabend and I had dinner at Brennan's, then we walked over to show the site." Kabacoff's sense of wonder is still evident here, finding a kindred spirit, at last. "He became very interested. For the first time in 10 years of trying, someone sent me a letter offering to lease this hotel, to pay us a basic rent and also guarantee the interest and the amount of the mortgage." Today, speaking from Sonesta headquarters in Boston, Sonnabend describes the situation this way: "Nobody was willing to commit to a hotel there. Kabacoff was the only one who believed in it. None of the big companies wanted to touch the French Quarter at all. It was not a place for a hotel, nor did the French Quarter have much of a future."

Early architect's drawing for the Royal Orleans.

With Kabacoff as tour guide, however, Sonnabend learned to tilt this picture just a little to the side - and see a design completely different. For one thing, he remembers, the whole idea just struck his fancy, along with the energy of its chief proponent and the caliber of its investors. A hotel in the French Quarter, he realized, could truly capture New Orleans as people imagined it, and thus be unique among similar properties in any other city. Finally and pragmatically, the site was "beautiful" to Sonnabend's trained eyes, ideally located with not one or two but three open streets.

Sonnabend's only set-in-stone condition was that the hotel be "of adequate size" for profitability, just a bit larger than Kabacoff and his proposal had in mind. Yet with the boost from HCA, the proclamation of faith in the long-rejected project, this struck all concerned as little more than a quibble. Certainly, if a larger hotel is required, a larger hotel will be built.

No one involved with creating the Royal Orleans expected absolutely smooth sailing - considering the French Quarter's long tradition of resisting any change and certain opposition from existing hotels, led time and again by the Roosevelt's politically connected Seymour Weiss. Yet on June 15, 1957, the front page of the *New Orleans States* could spotlight a photograph of the old St. Louis and the headline, "$6 Million Hotel Slated in Quarter." Quoting a joint statement from Edgar Stern and Roger Sonnabend, the *States* could report that after months of intensive negotiations, "a badly needed new hotel will become a reality in the heart of the Vieux Carre."

Artist's rendering of the hotel that came to be.

6

Grand By Design

That first triumphant announcement in the *States* contained a one-sentence aside that would prove prophetic: "Final design for the hotel is awaiting approval by the Vieux Carre Commission." Awaiting! That word became the status quo for the Royal Orleans in a series of battles that, at their bitterest, seemed to pit modernism against antiquity for the heart and soul of the French Quarter.

In the loudest of public hearings over this style of roof or that precise measurement of height, the lines were indeed being drawn between those who saw the Quarter as a slum with a heritage too glorious to change and those who recognized a dazzling touristic enterprise whose wealth had scarcily been tapped. Was the neighborhood better off with squalor and a series of historical markers? Or would it be better off, perhaps with fewer markers, but with a series of tourist attractions? Should it really become what the Quarter's many barroom wags would dismiss as a theme park for grownups? Just what should it become?

These questions would nag the developers of the Royal Orleans throughout the early years of construction and the almost immediate expansion. Yet this could occur only after they had taunted all the professionals called in to turn the legend of the St. Louis into a physical, and profitable, reality.

"The trick," recalls architect Arthur Q. Davis, "was to design a hotel that would have all the charm of the Vieux Carre, be reminiscent of the Quarter's historical background, and still be modern and efficient. We needed a hotel large enough to operate satisfactorily but one that retained the charm and intimacy of scale typical of the Quarter." On this subject, fellow architect Samuel Wilson Jr. chimes in: "Of course, we were greatly influenced by the style of the St. Louis Hotel. We gave the Royal Orleans the same height as the St. Louis had, a similar cornice line, a similar mass. The total exterior impact of the Royal Orleans is the same as that of the St. Louis."

Despite their persuasiveness, these comments on a grand (and ultimately successful) design downplay the amount of trial and error, even of soul-searching that went into the Royal Orleans' look and feel. Indeed, the mere presence of both Davis and Wilson on the same job is a clue that more than a few directions, and more than a few ironies, were at work on the construction site.

Davis was approached about handling the job by Edgar Stern Jr. His firm had never designed a hotel before, though several other of its public buildings had picked up important awards. The fact is, Davis was known to the Sterns primarily for designing the swimming pool at Longue Vue. "I'm sure you can do it," offered Edgar Jr.

It became clear to the architect quite quickly that a duplication of the old St. Louis was no more feasible than any "restoration" or "renovation" of a hotel that no longer stood. Something new was called for. But what? Clearing the site began to reveal an outline, even though the Sterns had used it most recently as a parking lot. At the back end, along

Chartres Street, stood a strip of granite arches with a two-story addition, the only surviving piece of the St. Louis. "That made them important and precious," says Davis. "To clear the site, we had them taken down piece by piece, numbered and stored. We not only used those arches themselves, precisely where they used to be - we used them as a model for all the new arches we put in along St. Louis Street."

The task before Davis was determined by Sonnabend and HCA: build a true French Quarter hotel of at least 350 rooms, a number dramatically higher than the 200 or so in the St. Louis. In order to set that many rooms into the same space - and stay within the Quarter's stiff height limitations - a series of courts came into being. Today, Davis describes the hotel's footprint as a "modified E sort of like an F, reminiscent of some of the older hotels in Paris such as the Georges V or a portion of the Ritz." This layout in courts not only met the technical requirements but allowed more exterior rooms overlooking the graceful rooftops of the French Quarter.

In addition to the irony of the fact that Davis had never designed a hotel before the Royal Orleans, there was the irony that he and his company were recognized almost exclusively for excellence in contemporary design. Even though he knew the French Quarter as a "special breed of cat," Davis in the early stages did suggest a series of designs that "might be a bit of a departure." None of these was able to win approval from the Vieux Carre Commission. Thus Davis was made architect of the interior, while the more traditional Wilson was brought on board to wrestle with the exterior challenges. The collaboration would work gloriously, not only on paper and in politics but in the hotel's later life.

With Wilson's mastery of historic Quarter architecture, a design came into being that would be a full five stories high yet give the impression, through the handling of upper windows, of being the St. Louis' original three. The Royal Orleans was given a flat roof, though without being asked Davis did design the roof to support an additional floor. That very floor would be needed less than two years after the hotel opened, sparking the Battle of the Mansard Roof. At least the physical support was there, designed in from Day One.

"I would have liked," Davis says three decades later, "to have seen us go a little farther toward creating some new forms and shapes in the French Quarter. But the Royal Orleans was the first. It could have set the direction in one way or the other. I think it established a standard that everybody had to keep up with if they wanted to compete."

That standard came into play dramatically in the hotel's interior design, a world relatively liberated from the requirements of preservationists. The interior had to work, to work in cooperation with the modern demands made of a luxury hotel and the traditional expectation inspired by the exterior. Yes, it simply had to work.

Davis' initial inclinations led him to a highly respected contemporary designer, who then produced a series of "really exciting concepts" led off by a double arched colonnade. However, the management at HCA felt these bold strokes might miss the mark in the Quarter - "too far out" is how Sonnabend described them - so the company sent in its own man from Miami. Eventually, after no small amount of impassioned discussion, an interior style for the hotel was found.

The lobby was a challenge, yet for many sets of eyes it would be the Royal Orleans' crowning glory. By definition, it would be an essential point of welcome to all guests and, if accepted as such, a profitable refuge for the people of New Orleans. Hotel lobbies can be magical places indeed, places not only of arrival and departure but of human contact, stylish imagery and social grace. The Royal Orleans had to achieve these goals in far less space than many of its predecessors in New York, London and Paris. So a multilevel lobby was designed, set off by a soul-stirring colonnade that repeats the exterior arches through splashes of tree-shimmered light. All this provided the impression of far more space than was present, not to mention a warm and welcoming area for meeting, for chatting over a drink, for sitting to watch the Quarter's tireless parade.

The layout of the guest rooms, like the choice of an interior designer, pitted Davis against HCA. The specifications from the management firm called for three basic room types, ranging from tiny spaces described as "salesmen's rooms" to two other types of increasing size - in spatial terms, robbing Peter to pay Paul.

"We were committed to a certain number of rooms to get the financing," Sonnabend explains. "We could have made the rooms all of the same size. But we chose to offset the corridor so rooms in the front have more space than rooms in the back. This way some rooms could be very special, so the hotel was able to offer them as being so." According to Sonnabend, this move also drew support from an age-old hotel tradition of building small rooms next to or across from large ones, rooms expressly for the maids, chauffeurs and other attendants who traditionally traveled with the upper crust. To Davis, however, this made little sense. Indeed these small rooms proved unpopular not only with salesmen but with just about everybody. Later, walls would be taken out to enlarge them.

Other touches added to the guest rooms seem almost quaint 30 years later, though at the time they were the subject of much boasting. Two terrycloth robes were kept in the closet of each suite - "one is a man's, the other a woman's," announced the earliest writings with a sense of almost sexual surprise. All rooms featured single thermostat controls that dialed heat or cooling to order, and there was ice water on tap in the bathrooms. Television sets were equipped with two extra channels for uninterrupted music, classical or popular.

Convention facilities were designed into the Royal Orleans, with a "special permanent registration facility adjacent to the front office in the lobby." Full theatrical lighting was provided, along with something called the Personal Motorola Paging Service for "busy convention secretaries or meeting

Full drawing of the Royal Orleans, as it took its place amid the buildings of the Quarter.

coordinators." Just as the hotel's sheer existence pointed the way to a tourism of the future, its earliest convention services show a sensitivity to what would become an important tourism segment. With the construction of a new Convention Center in the 1980s and its expansion in the 1990s, the wisdom of these preparations can be recognized even by the most casual of travelers.

Finally, there was the matter of food and beverage, a major portion not only of a luxury hotel's potential profit but of its special place in its community. In this new world of austerity and uniformity, anything is possible; but in the old world from which all grand hotels draw their inspiration the finest in food, wine, ambiance and service were essential parts of a hotel's identity. Even in the tradition of calling a restaurant simply the Dining Room and a bar simply the Main Bar, there was a mandate for uniqueness that set hotels apart for worldly travelers from every hemisphere. Once encountered, this uniqueness was something the traveler shared with all others who had encountered it and preached at the slightest opportunity to all who had not.

There were four outlets described in the Royal Orleans'

opening literature, of which three can be called precisely what one would expect of a luxury hotel anywhere. These were billed, naturally, as being perfect "to suit every mood and occasion." The Esplanade Room specialized in French cuisine in an elegant candlelit setting, while the Cafe Royale offered breakfast specialties at moderate prices and La Riviera served up a cafe-style experience of cocktails and snacks on the rooftop. The outlet that would provoke the loudest discussion in design was the one that, in the end, secured the hotel's reputation for culinary excellence, the Rib Room.

In the circle formed by Kabacoff, Sonnabend, Davis and others, there was serious discussion of creating a first-class Creole restaurant, one that would celebrate and even strive to advance the "cause" of New Orleans' rich native cuisine. Yet the fact that Antoine's was only steps from the hotel along St. Louis Street, and nearly a dozen Creole landmarks were within a brief stroll, convinced the circle that something quite different was needed.

"There were, at the start, different views about the Rib Room," concedes Sonnabend. "We had introduced the concept in our Boston hotel in 1951, but everybody in New Orleans was aghast because of the city's specialized cuisine. The locals thought it was absurd to have a restaurant specializing in prime beef, a restaurant that if anything was British! I persuaded them this was precisely what was required, rather than going head to head with the established Creole restaurants. As it turned out, the idea was so successful in New Orleans we built it into all our hotels for a long time after that."

As Arthur Davis says, "People just like to be in the Rib Room." To a large degree, it was Davis' achievement that people do. The idea was to take the Boston-British concept and interpret into something authentically New Orleans. This was carried out with columns of old brick, walls of old distressed cypress and light fixtures fashioned from old railroad headlights. These were marked with exotic Louisiana names, places the railroads used to run. "The use of materials," Davis explains, "and the details are the things that make it a unique room."

As time would pass, locals and visitors alike would recognize the entire Royal Orleans as unique. In fact, visitors saw this so rapidly that expansion plans were drawn up almost as soon as the property was operational. These plans proved a reminder that the battle between addressing the future and revering the past is an ongoing fact of French Quarter life.

This timeless French Quarter Scene shows the Royal Orleans in the early 1960s.

Corner of the new hotel, shortly after its grand opening.

7

Fire And Brimstone

ad the Royal Orleans been planned for any other neighborhood in New Orleans, it would have met everywhere the enthusiastic welcome given it in a newspaper editorial August 5, 1957. "All this is encouraging," the *Item* said. "New Orleans needs more hotels, not only for its tourists but also for its convention business. New Orleans' potential as a convention center is practically as big as we choose to make it." After observing that insufficient hotel space had long been the city's prime drawback in landing major conventions and itemizing revenues from the industry in 1957, the *Item* gave the planned hotel its unreserved blessing. "Convention dollars, it seems, get around town as fast as convention delegates. And they stay longer. And if more new hotels will bring more conventions, the more the merrier all around."

Yet the Royal Orleans wasn't planned for just any New Orleans neighborhood but for the French Quarter, where virtually anything a breeze couldn't blow away was viewed as a piece of history. As far back as 1936, there was even a regulatory body amended into Louisiana's constitution to oversee the Quarter - to protect its essence in the way later bodies would strive to protect the environment.

To the public at large, the Vieux Carre Commission seemed invaluable in pursuit of its mission, defined as the "preservation of the quaint and distinctive character" of the neighborhood. Its victories on a block to block, and sometimes building to building basis would culminate in 1968 with defeat of a proposed Riverfront Expressway that would have changed the French Quarter forever. But as the agency charged with approving every aspect of the Royal Orleans' exterior, and indeed every aspect of any change later on, the VCC would often seem to the partnership a panel of purists more concerned with keeping dust unmolested than with bringing the Quarter back to life.

Add to this confrontation the dizzying route through zoning boards and appeals courts - not to mention continual political sniping from Seymour Weiss of the Roosevelt - and the plans for the Royal Orleans at times seemed destined to remain plans. As Kabacoff observed of the French Quarter three decades later: "The people here will fight any change - good, bad or indifferent." There were days when even the partners must have wondered what kind of change they had in mind.

✿ ✿ ✿

Though plans to add a so-called mansard roof to the Royal Orleans in 1963 would generate the greatest controversy of all, even the empty site would be the subject of heated debate. As early as 1949, the basic scenario had begun to take shape, when Stern decided the land that would one day support his grand hotel should be used as a parking lot. The scenario included arming Kabacoff with blueprints and surveys, sending him forth into the halls of bureaucracy and letting him take the heat. Heat there was in 1949, even over plans to park cars on what was then a vacant lot.

Kabby argued before the city zoning board, whose approval Stern needed to push onward, that numerous officials had assured him such a facility was needed to relieve congestion around the gargantuan Civil Courts Building. Opposition to the plan, voiced at the hearing by residents, was that the lot "would be a nuisance for people living in the area because of noise, especially at night" and "would detract from the neighborhood and decrease property values considerably." These arguments would turn up again and again as the site evolved from parking lot to hotel, yet after studying both sides the board gave approval to Stern's initial plan.

The next major flourish of VCC activity occurred in November and December 1955, a period that takes in achitect Davis' memories of having designs rejected. At this point, Davis was still pursuing his dream of adding some "new forms" to the French Quarter. But it is clear that the commission did not share this dream. "The elevations were deemed not in character," the agency wrote to the partnership. "Story heights were not in scale with the story heights in the rest of the French Quarter." Only a month later, the VCC conceded that a building somewhat over 50 feet would not be objectionable, if it "meets all the other requirements of design of the Vieux Carre."

Intriguingly, there was a concern about the Royal Orleans quite apart from its appropriateness to one of America's most significant neighborhoods. The Vieux Carre Commission, with an intuition it would later set in stone, was fearful that if it approved demolition of present structures on the site and if the hotel agreement fell apart, the Quarter would have lost yet another preservation battle for nothing. The VCC even sent copies of the Stern-Kabacoff papers to the City Attorney's Office, to find out just how binding they were.

The City Attorney, after studying the documents, noted that they were far less hard-and-fast than agreements of such a serious nature tended to be, particularly agreements involving $6 million. The agreement put forward between the Stern real estate interests and the the Royal St. Louis Co. did not strike the City Attorney as "firm and binding," since it specified no specific type of building or damages if the building was not completed. "I might add as pure surmise," wrote the attorney, "that from the names of the corporations involved, it appears that perhaps all of these corporations may be owned by the same persons. That may be the reason they didn't make a firmer contract."

Eventually, these technical concerns were ironed out, as were nearly all the VCC's design considerations. The partnership's decision to bring in traditionalists Koch and Wilson to handle the exterior paid off, as did their arguments that the height of their proposed hotel was no greater than the original St. Louis. "Every new building in the Vieux Carre has to be considered individually," the commission ruled on Novermber 19, 1957. "It is felt that the design as approved will give a building that is truly French Quarter in design at a great expense to the applicant, and it will replace an open parking lot which has been one of our problems for years."

In a sense, the squabbles over the hotel's original design were only the opening round of a fight that escalated just two years after the Royal Orleans' gala opening on October 8, 1960. The property was praised by HCA patriarch A.M. Sonnabend during opening ceremonies as the equal of any in the world for beauty, efficiency and functional plant. "We are very proud," he said, flanked by Mrs. Stern and her son Edgar Jr., Mayor deLesseps Morrison and Rep. Hale Boggs, "of the fact that we now operate the Mayflower in Washington and the Plaza in New York, which we think are the two best hotels in the United States, and we are proud to add the Royal Orleans which we think now is one of the greatest hotels in the nation."

Tragically, Edgar Stern himself, the pragmatist who had sent forth Kabacoff on his visionary mission, had not lived to see the vision's first day in business.

Yet A.M. Sonnabend's pride was quickly borne out in profit. By 1962, the partners were already wishing they had built a bigger hotel - and wondering if there was something that could still be done about it. As it came to light that Arthur Davis had designed the top floor to support another story, a plan slowly took shape. Yet any plan would have to reckon with the Vieux Carre Commission, which would be asked to allow more height on a building many insisted was too high already.

The arguments that developed throughout the end of 1962 and a good portion of 1963 must have confused the casual observer beyond belief. Basically, the partnership proposed adding a mansard roof to the existing Royal Orleans - a roof section visually separate from the facade and swayed back a bit with graceful dormer windows. This penthouse level, with 52 additional guest rooms, was inspired by the architecture

Rare snowfall painted the hotel and the trees a strange color — white.

of Paris and was indeed very French Quarter. What's more, argued Wilson, it returned the hotel to its original appearance as designed by DePoilly and even to its "original" height, just under 91 feet.

The first problem was that Wilson's claims about the St. Louis' design flew in the face of surviving memory. Most memories of the old building drew upon the way it looked circa 1884, after alterations had given its facade a Victorian look. Photographs from the early 1900s showed sheet metal lintels above the third-floor windows and a heavy metal cornice at the top. Pointing to plans in the Notarial Archives (and also to the lobby mural by Boyd Cruise, based upon an old bank note), Wilson argued that DePoilly had carefully resurrected the style of Fontaine and Percier, architects for Napoleon. Both their buildings in Paris and his in New Orleans featured the mansard roof.

As for the issue of height, it placed a tangled web of evidence before both the city Zoning Board - which had set maximum height in the Quarter at just 50 feet - and the Vieux Carre Commission. All parties, at times simultaneously, seemed to be pointing to measurements from the past. But whose measurements, and measurements of just what, were to be considered? Seemingly, the Royal Orleans would be allowed to rise to the old St. Louis' "historic height." But just what height was that anyway?

As the technical arguments continued, the artistic debate did too. "The new mansard," Wilson claimed, "will give a rooftop of Paris look, blotting out, for instance, the unharmonious roof line of the former Civil Courts building across St. Louis St." Yet not everyone was convinced. John W. Lawrence, dean of the School of Architecture at Tulane University, sent the following telegram to the VCC: "Respectfully urge your condemnation of Royal Orleans proposal for additional story. This proposal profligate in its disdain of established zoning law. If approved privilege will have vanquished principal with grave future consequences."

However much truth there was in the dean's warning of "privilege over principal," the penthouse addition was approved by the Vieux Carre Commission in May 1963. The VCC had been persuaded by the arguments concerning the St. Louis' height - and far more importantly, by Wilson's claims that the mansard would be true to the look and feel of the French Quarter. In the end, declared VCC chairman I. William Ricciuti, it was not height but "aesthetic character" that mattered most. "It would be well," he wrote, in a letter protesting coverage in the Times-Picayune, "for all concerned to stop being swayed by the irresponsible mouthings of the incompetent and unqualified whose knowledge of the complex problems of historic preservation and of architecture is obviously small indeed."

✥ ✥ ✥

If at times the Royal Orleans and the Vieux Carre Commission seemed destined for confrontation, at least the commission's motives were clearly stated and essentially idealistic. Nothing of the sort could be said of the hotel's other nemesis throughout its early years, Seymour Weiss of the Roosevelt Hotel. It is impossible to find any motive other than greed - and fear of competition - for Weiss' repeated efforts to sabotage the Royal Orleans at every stage of its development.

To understand Weiss, one must understand something of his background. A barber from Abbeville, La., who worked at the Roosevelt in the 1920s, he had been elevated by Gov. Huey "Kingfish" Long to the role of confidant and campaign "treasurer." Enough of the treasure went Weiss' way that he later headed up a syndicate that purchased the hotel. After Long's assassination in the Capitol, Weiss went to the penitentiary as part of the Louisiana Scandals (in great company, along with the governor and the president of LSU), returning to run the Roosevelt as his private kingdom. Since Weiss owned New Orleans' best-known hotel, he tended to "own" the hospitality industry as well. What Seymour said had a way of going among the city's existing hotels.

Weiss' earliest assault on the Royal Orleans came during the investment phase. Time and again, as Kabacoff made his rounds from office to golf course, he was told what a rotten investment hotels were. When he inquired as to this information's source, he was most often told: Seymour Weiss. Profit? Never saw any! Occupancy? Never above 30 or 40 percent! Investment? Don't pour your money down the drain! It remained Kabacoff's contention three decades later that if any financial truth found its way into Weiss' reports, it was only by accident.

The second major assault came shortly after the Royal Orleans opened. In its role as management company, HCA decided to do something no other New Orleans hotel had done - advertise with billboards along the road in from the airport. No hotel had done it because Weiss didn't want any hotel to; he liked the fact that his Roosevelt was more famous than all the other hotels put together. When the Royal Orleans erected billboards, stressing its many comforts and services, Weiss engineered a vote to have it thrown out of the local hotel association.

"Our hotel became an individual player early on," Sonnabend remembers with satisfaction. "With our more modern marketing strategies, we made money our second year. It became silly for the hotel association after a while, so they invited us back. And before long, everybody was using billboards."

Olaf Lambert meets with his staff beside the pool.

8

Memories of Managing

grand hotel truly does draw its strength, its commitment, even its personality from the person charged with managing it. At this elevated level of service, the term "general manager" does not say nearly enough; only the traditional French "hotelier" seems to evoke the class-amidst-chaos that is this executive's daily gift and daily glory. Ever since its preparations for opening, the Royal Orleans has been served by a series of entrepreneurial hoteliers entirely capable of giving reality to Edgar Stern's dream: a world-class hotel in the heart of New Orleans.

These men were capable because they had studied world-class hotels both in theory and in operation, had risen through the ranks in precisely such hotels in Europe and in the United States. They could bring to the Royal Orleans not only the high standards HCA demanded from the start but the attitude, the vision that lay at the heart of grand hotels from London to Paris, New York to Singapore. Drawn from the small and close-knit brotherhood of true hoteliers, each of these general managers viewed the Royal Orleans as an opportunity to excel, both for himself and for those he gathered around him. Over time, each responded to the call of "bigger and better," yet all agree the Royal Orleans formed a special chapter in their lives - perhaps the best chapter of all.

It is a tribute to New Orleans' unique charm that despite globetrotting careers, four of the five managers who have run the Royal Orleans remain in the city. The only one to have left permanently, even for a place as seductive as San Francisco, speaks with so much nostalgia it's almost painful to listen. Together, their memories of managing give us a portrait of New Orleans through years of dramatic change, along with a reminder that the most important things here defy the passage of time.

❋ ❋ ❋

Olaf Lambert sits behind the desk of his sun-splashed French Quarter consulting office, dispensing telephone advice to friends and associates in the farflung corners of the world. Some of the advice is free, of course - you can't spend a lifetime in hospitality without being a little hospitable. Other advice is Lambert's bread and butter, the same mix of instinct and experience that helped him open the Royal Orleans 30 years earlier. Edgar Stern's hotel is the briefest stroll away, a stroll that Lambert makes often. Yet on this humid summer morning, the air conditioning is addictive, and Lambert is busy thinking about his father.

Stanislaus Lubienski was a prominent owner and operator of hotels in England and France, as well as in the United States and Canada. One result of his career was that Olaf was born in Sherfield-on-Lodden in Hampshire. Another was that this son grew up in his father's world, traveling from hotel to hotel in city after city. Lambert remembers his father as "a good operator rather than an entrepreneur or consultant" who taught him hands-on "a lot of practical things." Even with his own entrepreneurial tendencies, young Olaf realized he could achieve little in hotels without knowing the skills of a masterful waiter, a competent bellboy, an effective housekeeper.

By the time he was 18, Lambert has completed the four-year course in hotel and business administration at the Ecole de Commerce et d'Industrie Hotelier in Nice on the French Riviera. World War II put his career on hold, giving him a chance to fly with the Pathfinders in Britain's Royal Air Force and be shot down over the English Channel. During more than two years as a German prisoner of war, Lambert honed his management skills as head of an "Escape Committee."

The absence of reading materials sealed his fate as a lover of books for life. Isolated for three weeks with only Schopenhauer's "The Sex Life of a Toad," Lambert read the book 10 times - "not that I was crazy about toads!"

By the time he moved to New Orleans in 1959, the son of Stanilaus Lubienski had acquired a wife in New Zealand and a treasure chest of hotel experience in Istanbul, Berlin and beyond. When he heard from Roger Sonnabend's brother Paul that an HCA property was being built in New Orleans, Lambert asked to be considered for the GM's job. After all, he said, he spoke French and had a background in food and beverage, two things he figured would be essentials in the French Quarter. He was right about the second one, anyway.

Lambert arrived in the city to set up a pre-opening office in the courtyard behind WDSU. Though the hotel had barely risen out of the dirt, construction was not his responsibility. His challenge was choosing the people to handle its tasks once open - and by handling them correctly, creating its substance and its style. Department heads had to be selected first, including a young food and beverage director named Jim Nassikas; then the department heads had to fill in the blanks all down the line. Training got under way before there was a Royal Orleans to train in; under a succession of gifted managers, it never was allowed to stop.

"For HCA, we were a considerable training ground,"

Lambert remembers with satisfaction. "A lot of our people went to bigger properties and bigger jobs. Training was a priority. We recognized that what growing a small company needs is good management. We produced managers for HCA and for others. I think the numbers say a lot: We opened with 555 employees, and a year later we were at 400. Six years later, we had more than 100 who'd been there since opening. Some are still there now. As far as I'm concerned, I'm tickled pink to see people stay and to see people grow."

There were many challenges to staying and growing during Lambert's six years as general manager, one of the most memorable being the Deep South's struggle with integration. As a company managed from Boston, HCA took its place early among those pushing for equal rights - doing away with separate locker rooms and dining rooms for employees when all other New Orleans hotels said this would be impossible. Lambert recalls most vividly the decision to give each Royal Orleans employee dinner in the Rib Room on his or her birthday. "Many of our black employees had never eaten in a white restaurant," he says. "This showed them we weren't keeping a room segregrated."

Of all the people the hotel helped during this period, Lambert remembers one the best: a then-unrecognized (if later famous at Preservation Hall) piano player known as Sweet Emma. "She was a character all right, but she wasn't doing well financially," he says. "I told her that if she'd like to use the ballroom on Sundays free and pass the hat, that would be all right. That was the start of Jazz on a Sunday Afternoon, which went on for years."

Another meeting during Lambert's tenure produced jazz on a much larger scale, with the GM bringing in the man who produced the annual festival in Newport, R.I. "I knew about Newport," Lambert remembers. "And I wondered why in the hell people had to go to Newport when New Orleans is the city of jazz!" From that small meeting in the hotel's Pipkin Room, the New Orleans Jazz and Heritage Festival was born.

Jim Nassikas shares a glass of wine with his boss,
Olaf Lambert.

❈ ❈ ❈

"My years at the Royal Orleans were the most positive, enjoyable, personally stimulating and soul-nourishing experience I've ever had in a hotel. There was a great feeling of being a family there."

The speaker is Jim Nassikas, the food and beverage director under Olaf Lambert who stepped into the top job when New York's 2,000-room Loew's Americana lured his boss away in 1965. As a child of Greek immigrants born in New Hampshire, Nassikas too would answer the call of an even greater challenge, opening the posh Stanford Court in San Francisco and staying on as a resident of Marin County. Yet to hear him speak, it is obvious that the song "Do You Know What It Means to Miss New Orleans" applies to him. Nassikas could never really leave his heart in San Francisco, because he'd already left it in New Orleans.

Actually, Nassikas was an integral part of the Royal Orleans before it opened its doors. For three years he had been overseeeing food and beverage for the entire HCA company and had helped flesh out all the restaurants and bars put in place in the Crescent City. He hadn't particularly planned on leaving his corporate job, and certainly hadn't planned on spending the best years of his life in New Orleans. "I came to get these restaurants under way," says Nassikas, his voice clinging to the softest New England accent. "But one thing led to another. I was traveling back and forth so much, I finally took up residence preparing for the opening."

The position of New Orleans food and beverage director set him on the threshold, it turned out, the very place HCA would look when Lambert told the Sonnabends he couldn't turn down a 2,000-room hotel. Of course, Nassikas' background was an asset as well: education at the University of New Hampshire followed by the Ecole Hoteliere de la Societe Suisse des Hotelieres in Lausanne, Switzerland, followed by several years in European hotels before being invited to join HCA. He had even left New Orleans for a time after getting the Royal Orleans up and running, managing food and beverage at the legendary Plaza in New York. When asked to return to New Orleans as general manager, the idea was one he could not resist.

Like Lambert before him, Nassikas remembers HCA's commitment to integration as the single most dramatic aspect of his three years as GM. In particular, he remembers the hotel's decision to allow black taxi drivers to line up outside to pick up guests - a decision that inspired white taxi drivers to refuse service at the property for several years. And he remembers hiring a young black woman to work in the hotel's accounting department: "It was like that fellow James Meredith going into Ole Miss."

Glitz and glitter were always a part of the GM's job at the Royal Orleans, particularly when Hollywood came to call. Jane Fonda and then-husband Roger Vadim, the avant garde French filmmaker, were VIPs, as were Natalie Wood and Robert Redford during filming of "This Property Is Condemned" and Charlton Heston during filming of "Number One." The latter film, ironically, was set against the early years of the New Orleans Saints, who in those days seemed removed from any title except derogatory ones.

Richard Widmark and Edward G. Robinson were among the celebrities to sign the guest book during Nassikas' reign, as was the entire cast of a movie dearest to any hotelier's heart. Arthur Hailey's bestseller "Hotel" was being filmed in the city, with Rod Taylor in the lead. The entire cast stayed at the Royal Orleans, and several key scenes were filmed there.

Perhaps this GM's most moving memory concerns a special guest at the still-new Jazzfest. New Orleans-born Louis Armstrong returned for what turned out to be his last hometown performance. "We had a beautiful ballroom party for him at midnight, with the Preservation Hall band and a lot of other jazz musicians," Nassikas recalls. "People had come from all over the world, and the governor sent a special award to Armstrong. He was very jovial, very amiable and happy. There was no bitterness of any kind, even though for most of his life it would have been against the law for him to stay in this hotel."

The first opportunity to lure Nassikas away from the Royal Orleans was HCA's own Royal Sonesta, being constructed nearby on Bourbon Street. He was asked to serve as opening GM of that property, a request that in corporate career terms would have been difficult to turn down. Taking several of his key department heads with him, he adjusted his focus down the street - until he got a call from Edgar Stern Jr.

Nassikas in one of the happiest moments of his career, welcoming "Satchmo" home to New Orleans.

Over the years, Nassikas and Stern had spoken of opening a hotel on their own. Particularly with Stern's interest in food and wine, it was a fantasy that would not die. "Jim," said Stern in 1968, "I think we've found it." The HCA manager flew to San Francisco, toured a rundown 1911 apartment building on Nob Hill behind the Mark Hopkins and near the original Fairmont. "Edgar," he said, "this could be a very, very successful venture." The dream of the Stanford Court was born.

Nassikas fulfilled his commitment to HCA by opening the Royal Sonesta, then headed west for a glistening career that included not only an equity position at the Stanford Court - "I became my own boss, and the compensation was a lot better" - but working with Stern to open the Deer Valley Ski Resort outside Salt Lake City. Still, even after more than two decades away from New Orleans, when asked to think of a grand hotel, Nassikas thinks first of the Royal Orleans.

"It was just a monumental achievement," he says. "Because of the Sterns, there was an enormous commitment to doing it right. That's what they wanted. And I think that's what they got."

Jim Nassikas, during his later years with the Stanford Court.

*VIP guests were often treated to this special
tribute by the staff.*

9

Years of Gold

ach of the early general mangers alluded in some way to the blessing of the hotel's profitability. To Nassikas, the Royal Orleans was "extremely well stabilized." Yet to anyone tempted to interpret this fact in purely numerical terms, its relevance to the daily act of serving guests must be emphasized. There was a freedom in all this profitability, a freedom to serve graciously, tirelessly and fearlessly, a freedom to be precisely what a hotel was meant to be.

Perhaps Archie Casbarian, the GM who succeeded Nassikas, expresses this fact most clearly: "We had the unique pleasure of not being concerned about sales. The place was always jumping. For the only time in my career, before or since, we could concentrate on what a hotel was really about - guest services. We could worry only about making people happy."

As the Royal Orleans approached its 10th anniversary, a definite maturity of vision had settled in. The naysayers had long ago given up. Indeed, the slow revitalization of the

French Quarter had begun. With the arrival of the Sonesta as new kid on the block, some of the pressure of uniqueness had commuted over to Bourbon Street. Even the Royal Orleans' balance sheets had found precisely that: a balance that was indisputably golden.

The place was more than a fluke, more than a novelty, more than a case of beginner's luck. From U.S. presidents to European royalty, bestselling novelists to kings and queens of show business, it was simply the only place in New Orleans to stay.

�֍   ✖   ✖

Archie Casbarian hailed from one of the few cities on earth to rival New Orleans for romance and sheer ethnic entanglement: the Mediterranean port of Alexandria. His years finding a place among that city's Egyptians, Italians, Maltese, British, Greeks, Diaspora Jews and fellow Armenians taught him much about the need for tolerance. Yet when the intolerant Gamal Abdel-Nasser came to power in Egypt and began arresting all non-Moslems, Casbarian's father knew enough to send him to Switzerland. At age 17, more for his safety than for his career, he was enrolled in Nassikas' alma mater, the Ecole Hoteliere in Lausanne.

Casbarian was back in Egypt, working at the Continental Savoy, when his family endured a full year working for his father's release from Nasser's prisons. With that release, the plan changed again: young Archie was sent to the United States, to the rigorous hotel program at Cornell University. Casbarian surrendered to the inevitable, still hoping to build his life in Europe and, if possible, home in Egypt.

Cornell did what at that time Cornell did best, funnelling Casbarian into the most significant hotel jobs. But they were hardly where he wanted to be: Los Angeles, Curacao, New York, Washington and Boston. HCA came into the picture early on, seeing in Casbarian a young executive on the fast track. At the request of Nassikas, who had known him at the Plaza, the company sent Casbarian to New Orleans as assistant general manager of the Royal Orleans. "I had heard so much about New Orleans and had never been here," he recalls. "I fell in love with the French Quarter the minute I saw it. And the Royal Orleans was magic to everybody. It had already launched many careers."

Long before Casbarian expected, Nassikas moved on to the Royal Sonesta and he at the age of 32 was given the Royal Orleans. It was the beginning of the time he describes, to the surprise of most who know him today, as the happiest of his life.

Recognizing with greater clarity than his predecessors the unique opportunity of having money in the bank, Casbarian embarked on a series of innovations large and small that had the effect of piling up still more money. A connoisseur of the perfect martini, he introduced oversized versions in frosted glasses served from rolling carts by attractive young ladies. He introduced the first of many food festivals, this one a Mexican fiesta in the Rib Room with imported mariachi band and consulting chefs from Mexico.

The hotel served its first Sunday brunch under Casbarian, along with its first flaming desserts and coffees in the Esplanade Lounge. The pool deck got new landscaping, as in a sense did the staff: the first of what became an annual costume change, quite the conversation piece among regulars.

A series of additional "firsts" did not so much reflect the times as brought the times to New Orleans. Casbarian introduced women employees to the male bastion of the front desk and appointed a woman assistant manager. As far as he knows, both of these moves were unique in the city at the time.

Some of Casbarian's most dramatic memories of the Royal Orleans concern one visit by President Richard Nixon and several by his original vice president, Spiro Agnew. The day of Nixon's arrival had been rehearsed down to the small

Archie Casbarian and Ron Pincus greet President Nixon in the center of the curbside chaos.

est detail, practically with written exams given employees by members of the Secret Service. The president was to step out of his limousine onto the curb, be greeted by Casbarian and be shown to the elevator. That would be that.

Yet at the moment all this was supposed to take place, surrounded by a swarm of dark-suited agents with walkie-talkies abuzz, the President chose to climb out on the street side of his limo and virtually disappear into the public. All the calm from the rehearsals crumbled and the only task became: Get Nixon inside! Finally, Casbarian was able to shake the president's hand and escort him to the elevator. "I was struck," he remembers, "surrounded by all these people going nuts, by how cool, calm and collected this guy was."

Agnew paid several visits to the Royal Orleans, often adopting Casbarian's office as a place to sit, chat and unwind. Casbarian helped him make tennis reservations, with the vice president reciprocating with an open-ended offer of assistance. Sure, Casbarian remembers thinking, as if I'm ever going to call!

A short time after one of Agnew's stays, however, a problem arose over the immigration of Casbarian's parents from the city they now called home, Beirut. The Lebanese jewel was beginning to disintegrate into the hell it would remain for years; yet the immigration request seemed stalled indefinitely. Red tape swirled upward with every necessary step, while the clock ticked dangerously in Beirut. "It was my secretary who encouraged me to call Agnew, and at first I didn't want to," says Casbarian. "I didn't even know how you went about calling the vice president, but she got him right on the line."

The next day in Beirut, the U.S. ambassador called Casbarian's parents to say the process was moving right along. Soon, they were safely on American soil. The ambassador let on that he had received plenty of calls about plenty of immigration cases, but never before one from the vice president of the United States.

In the end, Casbarian was presented with a decision similar to the one that had faced Nassikas. What to make of this hotel life? Do you rise in the corporate structure, go from hotel to hotel? Do you continue to be someone else's golden boy, or do you do something for yourself? Do you go wherever the next posting is or stay in the one city you love above all others?

In Casbarian's case, love of New Orleans was made tangible by his love for one of its daughters, his wife Jane. Together, they chose to remain. They chose to raise their children not only in New Orleans but in the French Quarter. They chose to leave the hotel business and resurrect Arnaud's Restaurant, a long-overdue testiment to its founder, Arnaud Cazenave. They chose a new life's work. Yet even in this, the Royal Orleans played an early and essential role.

"If I look back on my career," Casbarian says, "my fondest memories would be of this hotel. One day, in fact, the woman who would become my wife was a guest on the pool deck. I saw her, arranged for an introduction, and the rest is history."

❀ ❀ ❀

History was precisely what Casbarian's successor would both see and oversee - and not just because Ron Pincus and his wife Anne would meet at the Royal Orleans. Describing himself as different in personality from his three predecessors, Pincus would not only build on their achievements but find a security and a satisfaction in running the hotel that kept him there 21 years - an unbelievable 19 as vice president and general manager. Though each GM left his imprint in ways discernible today, Pincus' ideas and energies must be considered special because they held sway for so long. "I have very strong personal feelings for every brick and piece of furniture at the Royal Orleans," Pincus says now, "but even more for the people. When I left it was with great remorse, and with tears in my eyes."

Pincus, a native of Florida, first tasted the pleasures of New Orleans during an Army posting at Camp Leroy Johnson. During that period, as he contemplated careers in many fields but leaned toward none, he remembers walking through the Royal Orleans on the night it opened and thinking, "What a beautiful, beautiful place!"

Recalled into the Army during the Berlin Crisis, Pincus settled in the nation's capital and eventually embarked on preparations to become a CPA. His college degree was in accounting, though he thought of this career with no more enthusiasm than he thought of any other. Right before he was to sit for the CPA exam, he had a crisis of his own. "Do I really want to do this for the rest of my life?" The answer, without question, was No.

Without any understanding of what fate had in store, Pincus accepted a trainee's position at HCA's legendary Mayflower Hotel in Washington. The job was in the financial office, where his college work might do him some good. But whatever he felt about the opportunity had as much to do with his childhood as with any curriculum. "I'd always loved hotels," recalls Pincus. "When I was a child, my father traveled a lot and sometimes he'd take me with him. As soon as they said the job was in a hotel, I knew that was what I was destined for."

Is Ron Pincus greeting western star Chill Wills or dancing with him?

Destiny spoke its piece quickly. The No. 2 man in the control office, Archie Casbarian, headed down to New Orleans as assistant to Jim Nassikas and quickly moved up to general manager. To be his assistant, Casbarian sent for the man he'd first seen as a trainee. And when Casbarian himself moved on, Pincus rose up behind him.

One of the main themes of the next 19 years was stability within change, that necessity in modern business life. Above all, it was Pincus' financial and emotional mission to maintain the great hotel though a series of ownership changes that normally would have threatened his career and even the status of the Royal Orleans. The fact that both he and the hotel remained "constants" in each equation is a tribute to Pincus' sense of calm, not to mention his executive survival skills.

By the early 1970s, HCA's fire for hotels began to wane under financial pressure. Now using "Sonesta" as its corporate identity, it sold the Royal Orleans to an English company named Lex Service Group - which was looking to expand its varied holdings in the United States. Before Lex itself would back out of hotels, it would give Pincus eight solid years of support. This included advanced management courses in London taught by Harvard professors flown in for the day or even the hour. At one point, Pincus was offered the presidency of Lex, but the fact this would have meant leaving New Orleans convinced him to decline. His far greater desire, by this time, was quite different: to own the Royal Orleans.

After sensing that Lex was transferring its commitment from hotels to electronics and receiving permission to submit the first bid, Pincus put together an investor group to make the purchase. Just days before the presentation in London, however, word came that someone else within the company had worked out a sale to Dunfey Hotels. The letter of agreement had already been signed. "I came that close," Pincus says today, expressing the closest thing to regret likely to turn up in his voice.

Years later, the disappointment has subsided, and Pincus

speaks mostly of the first-class trip to Europe he and his wife were given by the chairman of Lex. The trip was terrific, he remembers, but not nearly as terrific as the thing Pincus the tennis buff had always wanted: tickets to the championships at Wimbledon.

Unbelievably, the general manager was contracted to stay on by Dunfey, a hotel company that had taken the Royal Orleans to upgrade its corporate image. This it and Pincus managed to do, throughout Dunfey's purchase of Omni Hotels and its eventual assumption of the Omni name. All this led, in the 1980s, to Omni's acquisition by Wharf (Holdings) Limited of Hong Kong and the beginning of a new era.

By this time, Pincus was managing director of the Royal Orleans and Omni's regional vice president of operations. He had no particular interest in moving on, no particular passion to conquer new worlds. But then the Monteleone called.

Pincus' son Matthew welcomes canine VIP Lassie in the movie star's Royal Orleans suite.

A much older French Quarter hotel, built in the late 19th century, the Monteleone offered Pincus a 10-year financial package he could not refuse. Within months, he convinced his new bosses the hotel needed a dizzying series of renovations. These required a firm hand connected to an accountant's brain. Both were needed to steer the renovations clear of disasters financial and otherwise.

Today, in his office at the Monteleone, Pincus' thoughts sometimes drift a few blocks deeper into the French Quarter, to the hotel that was his home for 21 years. He doesn't think about the celebrities, though: not about Nixon or Agnew, not about Bob Hope or King Hussein, not about the VIPs he greeted almost daily. He thinks mostly of the people who worked for him, people he watched grow, people whose families became an extension of himself. He still hopes for good on their behalf, and for the hotel they make happen daily without him.

"What was the golden glow of the Royal Orleans?" Pincus asks himself. "I honestly can't tell you." He pauses, then pushes ahead. "Maybe it's a certain time in your life, as it was for me. Maybe it's a certain time in this city's life, when the Royal Orleans was the only game in town. And maybe it was the people who worked there. Those people were very proud of working there. They didn't really know what luxury was, but it was continually imbued in them that they were working in a very special place. In the end, it worked. Because of them, the Royal Orleans became a luxury hotel."

*To this day, the Rib Room remains a
major attraction for locals.*

10

Into the Future

In the fall of 1990, Omni faced a major challenge - replacing a general manager whose longevity in the job was greater than that of all his predecessors. To the staff, and indeed to the people of New Orleans, Ron Pincus had been the Royal Orleans for so long that deciding who would follow him was an intimidating task from the start.

Several other pieces to the puzzle had changed during Pincus' tenure that made finding the right successor crucial. Since the day of its opening, the hotel had prided itself on being not just the best in its class in New Orleans but the only one in its class: a modern hotel with Old World reverence for amenities and personal service. Spurred by the 1984 World's Fair, however, at least four or five other hotels had opened in the city capable of convincing guests they were in the same league. In business, the arrival of competition is hardly the end of the story; but it is the end of one chapter and the beginning of another. For the Omni Royal Orleans, improvements of facilities became constant. Greater awareness of the marketplace became a daily challenge, and an increasingly sophisticated appeal to that marketplace became a necessity. The days of graciously playing host to the world had in one sense come to an end; the days of aggressively seeking the honor of playing host had begun.

As Omni went forth into the industry with its search, it knew well that times had changed - both in New Orleans and in the fabric of hospitality itself. One change etched clearly by the company's eventual choice was the evolution away from dependence on European training and experience. Olaf Lambert's background was primarily European, as were Nassikas' and Casbarian's. Yet during their years at the Royal Orleans, not only had the Cornell hotel program come to be recognized as equaling Europe's best but it had spun off similar departments at universities across the United States. Tourism was becoming bigger business all the time: why shouldn't American universities train students for such a challenge?

Omni's choice of the GM who would guide the Royal Orleans into the future turned out to be someone who understood its past with clarity yet had learned his profession in the rough-and-tumble atmosphere of American competition. For the first time, the top job at New Orleans' top hotel would be held by a New Orleanian.

❈ ❈ ❈

Gary Froeba remembers working at a Holiday Inn between business management courses at the University of New Orleans. He was doing it all at that time: cooking in the kitchen, holding down the front desk, tending bar, even handling night audit. Early one New Year's Eve, the hotel's general manager asked him to show him around the French Quarter. As part of the tour, Froeba showed his boss the one place that impressed in a way quite different from any other: the Royal Orleans.

"Wouldn't it be great to run this hotel one day?" the student worker asked with excitement.

"It sure would be," his general manager replied.

The Royal Orleans remained on Froeba's mind over the years - though he insists he never knew he'd return to New Orleans at all, much less to his favorite hotel. He thought of his Brother Martin High School senior prom, held in the hotel's Grand Ballroom. He thought of the times he spent in the hotel's restaurants and lounges courting Lynne Kaiser, who became his fiancee and later his wife and later the mother of his children. Yet each of these memories had to take its place against the backdrop of a busy and increasingly successful career.

The Brock Hotel Corporation was Froeba's home for 13 years, managing a series of properties in New Orleans and then as general manager of two hotels in Columbia, Mo. In 1981, Brock named him General Manager of the Year.

Tourism's big time called Froeba in 1985, luring him away from this company to serve as general manager of the Americana Dutch Resort (which became the independent Grosvenor Resort) in Lake Buena Vista, Fla. This was one of the "official hotels" of Walt Disney World, with all that designation entailed: high glitter, high visibility, high profit. Froeba's work experience served him well, as he guided the resort through an $8.5 million renovation and increased its annual revenues from $15 million to $25 million. These were the measuring sticks by which the hotelier of the future would be judged, and Froeba was judged a success.

When Omni called him about the Royal Orleans, Froeba wasn't sure he was interested. The verve of Orlando's hospitality industry was addictive; it seemed as though real tourism existed nowhere else on earth. Besides, Orlando was treating him well, asking him to serve as president of its hotel-motel association, as vice president of its convention and visitors bureau, as adjunct professor of its community college. Froeba was inclined to keep all he had - until he and his wife let Omni talk them into spending a weekend at the Royal Orleans. That brought back too many memories, too many memories to resist. Froeba traded his mouse ears for a Mardi Gras mask and packed for the emotional trip home.

❈ ❈ ❈

"I see my role as continuing to position the hotel above the cluster of luxury hotels," Froeba says, sitting in his office today, "to set a distance between them and us in terms of amenities, service and ambiance. We have the best address in town, but we need to introduce new ideas and new ways of

A reunion of the four GMs who stayed in New Orleans: Froeba, Pincus, Casbarian and Lambert.

doing things to a work force that has done things certain ways for 30 years. My mission also is to keep this hotel part of the fabric of our history, and that's a tough task in today's market."

It was clear the Royal Orleans staff wanted a GM who knew what was going on in each department, who cared about people's jobs and even their personal lives, who knew when to push and when to back off, who was demanding but kept everything running crisply, and who was savvy enough financially to assure everyone a dependable income. With no thoughts of reinventing the wheel - knowing he had a great one already - Froeba worked to incorporate his staff's vision into the one he had developed for himself. In time, the unavoidable fear of change began to fade away.

"When the employees found out I'd gone to Brother Martin and UNO, that I knew what Mardi Gras was all about, that I knew they ate red beans and rice every Monday and that I knew how to spell Tchoupitoulas Street, they were very relieved," Froeba recalls. "To do what you need to do in this business, you must have the support of your staff."

The future of the Royal Orleans is not only Froeba's corporate mandate, it's his personal and professional fascination. Yet he approaches that future the only way it can be approached, as the wisest New Orleanians have always understood: from the richness of the past. Renovations? Certainly. Adjustments? When necessary. New ideas? When effective. But none of these must be allowed to change the essence of the Royal Orleans, or of the city it calls home.

"The future is in our past," Froeba says with simplicity. "That part never goes away. This hotel will always be a great luxury hotel. That's the way it was in the grandest days of New Orleans. And that's the way it will remain."

Days in the Life

*Remembering the Royal Orleans, shown here in the 1960s,
is remembering New Orleans.*

*At 7 feet 8 inches tall, John the doorman was a landmark
unto himself in the mid '60s.*

11

Autumn Voices

Like any business, a hotel is built of many parts. Yet a hotel is more than the sum of these parts. Perhaps it's the fact that what it offers is life itself, in the form of shelter and sustenance. Perhaps it's the the fact that it must be a small city, a community of diverse goods and services, to handle the jobs required of it. And perhaps it's the fact that its people - people who over the years are both citizens of a city and members of an extended family - give of their lives in a place through which others merely pass. Yes, a hotel is more than the sum of its parts, but never more than the sum of its people.

On an autumn afternoon, as the first promise of cool weather moved through the streets of the French Quarter, a handful of these people gathered in a Royal Orleans meeting room. Retired, semi-retired and still employed, they were above all happy to see each other. Yet as the afternoon lengthened, their stories moved from catching up to looking back, to their memories of others not at that table. The faces of guests young and old flashed before their eyes, into and out of their stories. And for all the pain of time's passage, each could smile at years full of moments he or she had given to the Royal Orleans.

✿ ✿ ✿

If a hotel's duty is dispensing rooms to weary travelers, Jackie Janneck is a room dispenser par excellence. Though she now serves as Guest Services Manager, she spent most of her quarter-century at the Royal Orleans running the front office. Deciding who got what room was her affair - and in a hotel that was full so much of the time, deciding who got what (and sometimes who got nothing) was more than a clerical exercise. It was a heartstopping mix of careful planning and rolling the dice.

The Front Office and its primary public outlet, the Front Desk, are essential to the experience of any hotel. It is the first stop for every guest, and the only official stop made by many. If a guest never dines in the hotel's restaurants, never orders room service, never catches a housekeeper turning down his bed and never calls an engineer to adjust the air conditioning, the person who checks him in and out becomes the hotel to him. It was Jackie Janneck's job to make those brief encounters superlative. Her mission each night was to fill every room without sending a single soul away, and to do it all with courtesy and respect.

"I remember oodles of celebrities," she says, letting on that having "rooms to let" does have its perks. "We had the king of Norway, the presidents of Panama and Romania, and Miss Lillian Carter, President Carter's mother. Oh, and we had Michael Jackson, here with his brothers, his dad and his tutor. He was just a little fella back then." Following a certain track, she ponders then moves on. "The Rolling Stones twice, the Jefferson Airplane, Zsa Zsa Gabor and Eva Gabor, Paul Newman... I remember the day Paul Newman had lunch in the Rib Room. Well, the women who worked here never even passed through the Rib Room. That day, every single one of them found some excuse to at least peak in. And then there was this sheik...

"Of Araby," Bill Neff chimes in, recalling the old song.

"Yeah, from someplace," says Jackie, remembering the way the sheik's bodyguard had welcomed the room service waiter with an Uzi.

❋ ❋ ❋

If anyone worked with Jackie Janneck it was Bill Neff - though sometimes it seemed he worked against her. As a salesman for the hotel's goods and services, finally as its director of sales, it was his job to pull in every piece of business that strolled by. Today, semi-retired, Neff is still a

Jazz bands such as the famed Olympia often keep time in the Royal Orleans lobby.

salesman: you meet him and you want to buy something. This must have been true during his 23 years with the Royal Orleans, because a lot of people bought a whole lot. If it was occasionally more than Jackie Janneck had to sell, that too was part of the game.

"It's like the airlines," Neff explains. "If they sold every seat just once, they'd fly empty most of the time. So they sell each seat several times and then it works out, usually. The airlines have all this scientific research to tell them what to do. In hotels, you can spend all the money in the world but no one can tell you what'll happen. Sometimes you can book 150 over and still have empty rooms. Another time you take one extra reservation and that guy shows up."

As a "people person" in a "people business," Neff is the first to say it's people that make hotel sales satisfying. But it's also people who make it a challenge. Endless people leaving endless phone message. Endless people you've never met and yet are compelled to court.

"Like one time," he remembers, "I got this message to 'Call Mr. Bishop in St. Louis.' So I did and we talked and through the whole conversation I kept saying, 'Yes, Mr. Bishop' and 'No, Mr. Bishop.' When I finally went to fill in our reservation form, I asked this guy for his full name. He said, "I'm Archbishop William Cody of St. Louis." Well, I felt like an idiot, but it must have been all right. When Cody was appointed archbishop in New Orleans, he became quite a client. He had all kinds of functions here."

❈ ❈ ❈

"Overbooked?" breathes restaurateur Marc Turk, who worked at the Front Desk and later in sales for the Royal Orleans. "Sure, we were overbooked sometimes. And like any other hotel, there were some nights we 'walked' guests to other hotels around the city." He smiles. "But I'll bet we're the only hotel that ever walked a bus to the Broadwater Beach in Biloxi!" He pauses to let the notion sink in, then continues. "When we looked at the night's reservations, we all said a novena they wouldn't all show up. But they did. So when that bus pulled up, I caught the escort just as she stepped out, turned her right around and marched her right back on the bus. I just kept talking and talking, about what good care we were going to take of them."

Turk sent a hotel representative with the bus to Biloxi, giving the group a tour of NASA test facilities and providing free cocktail parties for each and every dull moment. "When that group got back the next day," says Turk, "they said they'd never been treated so royally and never been shown such a great time." A devilish smile works its way in. "And we still made $3 profit on each room."

Like any hotel employee, Turk takes as a matter of course an extended list of weird requests. Basically, guests ask for so many strange things that after a while nothing seems strange. Yet half the people around the table brightened at the memory of the tycoon named McCarthy who insisted upon sending a live turkey wearing a Santa beard and a rhinestone necklace to the Uptown home of restaurateur Adelaide Brennan. It is a story only Marc Turk can tell - especially since he was the delivery man.

"The idea was, you never say No to a guest," Turk explains. "So we found this live turkey somewhere in Mississippi, got the rhinestone necklace, the beard and some jingle bells. But then no taxi would take us Uptown. Mr. McCarthy offered us his big old Rolls, so that's what we took, driving a Rolls through the streets of New Orleans with a live turkey in the back. Naturally, we saw everybody we knew on that trip! We got the turkey in the gate at Adelaide's, but here around the bend come two great big labrador retrievers. That bird took off to the end of its leash, and let go in more ways than one.

"The maid informed us that Adelaide wasn't coming to the door to accept a live turkey. And besides, she told us, she didn't think Adelaide was going to want it after what it just did to her newly painted veranda. Finally, we hooked the turkey on an umbrella stand and ran."

The thing is, says Turk, you never really know what people are going to do, what they really want from you or how they're going to react to what you give them. This element of the unknown made "working with the public" a great deal more stressful than it is depicted in recruiting ads for the hospitality industry.

"We walked the brother of the *Times-Picayune's* publisher once," he says, "and then got to read all about it on the next day's front page. One man from the Southern Baptist Convention, when we tried to walk him, just went on down to a sofa in the lobby and began to undress. We figured we had to do something for him. Another guest grabbed a clerk across the Front Desk, holding him there all stretched out with his tie." Turk pauses. "That's when we started wearing clip-ons. And then there was the guy who went after me with a tennis racket. I don't know what made me come out to talk to him, but he chased me all the way down the lobby toward the ballroom."

✪ ✪ ✪

Joe Bergeron joined the Royal Orleans in 1964, starting at the Front Desk. The main thing he remembers about those days was naked people getting locked out of their rooms in the night and waving to him from the elevator for help. Night shifts are like that.

Rather quickly, Bergeron became a bellman - perhaps because he didn't want to get chased with a tennis racket, perhaps because he figured out where the money was. He joined the fraternity in any hotel that holds the patent on knowing everything in the house and making a few bucks on nearly all of it. It is no coincidence that bellmen in books and movies are always colorful, usually a tad shady and invariably important to the plot. Bergeron belies the shady part but certainly evokes the well-choreographed service that is his elite brotherhood's stock in trade.

"The good part about my job," he says, "is that you never have to say No to a guest. You're there to please and it's so easy. What can they expect of you but service?" He thinks a bit about the coin's other side. "The biggest challenge is when you have plenty of check-ins. It's like bananas, they come in bunches. The important thing is making people think you're not rushing them, even when you are. The trick is to stay with the guest the whole time you're taking his bags to the room, not sending him on ahead. That way you can spend the whole time telling him about the hotel, and then in the room explain all about the TV, the hair dryer and the air conditioner. That way, you can get on down to the lobby and serve the next guest checking in."

Asked to describe the most colorful bellman he ever worked alongside, Bergeron smiles. He mentions the name and everyone around the table smiles too. "You see," he says, "this guy ran a small drugstore downstairs, right out of his locker. Whether it was a couple aspirin or a bottle of whiskey, he could sell it to you. The stores were all closed at night, you see. If he didn't have it in his locker, you couldn't get it."

❋ ❋ ❋

Jaunelle Lane doesn't mind if you call her "feisty" or "outspoken." She admits she's been called much worse by the men who have passed through the Royal Orleans as her bosses. Yet since a month after the hotel opened its doors in 1960, she has been passionately concerned with making the place look its best. In fact, when she moved into her present position in 1965, she figured that her housekeepers were just about the only essential people in the operation.

"The sales director can sell his heart out," she observes with pragmatism, "but if the housekeeper doesn't clean things, he's got nothing to sell. We can make or break the hotel. People in housekeeping hold the most important positions. I figure the building belongs to me when I'm here. I owe something to this building. I figure: If I take care of the building, the building will take care of me."

As she moved into housekeeping from supervising the hotel's cashiers, Ms. Lane's outlook is more managerial than domestic; yet her system has clearly worked. Several of her housekeepers have kept their jobs for three decades. And even after her own recent illness, Jaunelle Lane insists she's not going anywhere.

Gloria Breaux is a housekeeper. When she isn't helping manage the army that takes on the guest rooms each day, she is herself doing precisely that. Though her work is largely unheralded and the rewards at times seem slim, housekeepers like Gloria are essential parts of what a grand hotel is. Nothing would be possible without their labors. From the careful cleaning of rooms between one guest and the next to the graceful "turndown service" the Royal Orleans offers as a gift in the night, housekeepers are the unsung heroines who hold the puzzle together.

"The biggest challenge is satisfying guests," she says, knowing that's a mouthful, "especially since there's no two guests that are alike. And people sometimes think we never meet the guests - you know, just sneak in and change the sheets and the towels. But we meet the guests quite a lot and have to treat them special, just like everybody else working here." Sometimes, being sweet comes naturally; other times it's a stretch.

"We have one of our ladies, you know, she sings a lot of church songs while she moves around and while she works. Every time you run into her, there she is just singing some church song. Well, one time she knocked on a door and this nude guy said, 'Come on in.' She just gave him a little prayer and then told him why he should put on some clothes."

Rock groups sometimes are considered housekeeping challenges, especially those with destructive reputations to maintain. But Gloria Breaux remembers her rockers fondly, from Mick Jagger and his Rolling Stones to members of that group whose name she could never catch no matter how many times they pronounced it: Sha Na Na. A slightly larger challenge was presented by her canine and feline guests, including Lassie, Benji and Morris the cat. Of course, for Gloria Breaux, even cleaning up after them was all in a day's work.

❖ ❖ ❖

In the mad quest for French Quarter parking, sometimes it is indeed not what you know but who you know - particularly if you know Larry. Since the year before the Royal Orleans opened, knowing Larry Johnson, and having him recognize your car, has been one of the surest methods of parking known to man at his most frazzled. "If you know Larry in the garage," goes the longtime saying, "you can get into the garage."

Larry Johnson is nothing less than the Royal Orleans' most tenured employee, the one honored to cut the hotel's cake each year on its "birthday." He started to work not on that birthday but a full year before that, when there existed no hotel at all.

Larry began as a "hiker," one of the guys who dash about searching for your car then deliver it to you in hopes of a tip. Honestly, he figured he'd put in a year and move on. Today, he is the "postman," who doesn't deliver mail but does direct many hikers to keep things moving in the garage. As postman, he is also the one who decides whose car gets in and whose car is turned away as his spaces dwindle to zero. Like so many others in a great hotel, Larry is essentially in inventory management. Yet also like so many others, he considers himself in guest service.

*Pretty maids all in a row? No, simply the
champagne servers at a Royal Orleans reception.*

"Don't fight the customers," he says when asked his
secret, the briefest smile flickering across his lips. "If you
fight them, they're going to win anyway. You know, what
service is is being treated special - being treated like you're
somebody special. Some people say everybody's the same,
but that's not at all what people want. They just want to be
treated special."

❀ ❀ ❀

"They used to call it Fisher's Country Club." The man
speaking is Ernst Fisher, who ought to know. And the "country club" is the Rib Room, the restaurant he has not only
managed since coming to New Orleans in 1969 but has
embodied in style and personality. At peak times in the local

economy, executives made it virtually their lunch room - lured by the terrific prime rib and lubricated by the huge martinis. Despite the Rib Room's current awards and immense popularity, Fisher must be excused a few musings about the past. At the table this autumn afternoon, it goes with the territory.

"I started on the day of Nixon's inauguration," the Austrian-born maitre d' recalls. "I was planning to stay here two years, maximum, and then leave for San Francisco. But I'm still here. You know, when I started, people just didn't go to hotel restaurants in New Orleans, especially at lunch. They had a reputation for not being so good, and there were so many places to choose from. But the Rib Room changed all that."

The martinis were one thing that pushed the change through, and the fact that the restaurant didn't feel part of the hotel was another. Still another was the regularity with which celebrities could be spotted at its tables, a byproduct of that luxury hotel the Rib Room didn't wish to feel part of.

Fisher in particular remembers a dinner with journalist David Brinkley, who was heading into Plaquemines Parish the next day to interview segregationist Leander Perez. Brinkley admitted to fear he might never make it out. The maitre d' remembers catering to Luciano Pavarotti early in his career, making him a clear consomme he requested for his voice. And he remembers taking care of the Rolling Stones, worrying all the while he'd make them late for their concert in the Superdome. "Don't worry," they said. "The concert starts when we get there."

As Fisher's grandfather worked at the operahouse in Vienna, opera stars were special favorites of his. He loves to remember surprising Wagnerian soprano Birgit Nilsson by addressing her in Swedish, then explaining that his wife is Swedish. He also loves remembering the way she downed prime rib and three beers. Yet sports figures also were a thrill for Fisher, a list led off by boxers. Max Schmelling, the German great from the 1930s, was amazed Fisher recognized him. Others not so hard to recognize included Floyd Patterson, Muhammad Ali and Larry Holmes, along with wild-haired promoter Don King and tireless ring commentator Howard Cosell.

Sharing in all of Fisher's memories, and having quite a few of his own, is assistant manager Dalton Milton. Starting as a busboy in 1960, Milton came up through the ranks, with stops for such jobs as service waiter and bartender. He listens rather quietly to Fisher's stories, then turns the anecdotes into law.

"Service is the name of the game," he muses on his 30-plus years in the Rib Room. "It sounds easy on paper when you're at a meeting. But then, when it's showtime, you throw the book away. You have to have a plan, but you have to be ready and able to deviate from it." Milton smiles, as though there's a secret aching to be told. "You know, when you're in a dining room 12 or 15 hours a day and you see all that goes on, you can tell how much a guy is going to tip before he orders a Coca-Cola. So you just try and please everybody."

❧ ❧ ❧

Harold Sage lives up to his last name. As the employee most likely to have walked into, peered into or crawled into every corner and crevice of the Royal Orleans over 28 years, he speaks of its physical plant as though it were alive. Indeed, as Sage would surely tell you, a hotel building is alive - a sometimes stubborn body that needs near-constant pampering and encouragement. Over the years, when bits of the body rebelled, it was most often Sage who had to coast those bits into activity. Though now retired, the chief engineer still dons the uniform on regular occasions and comes on in to help out.

As befits a worker seldom called when everything is okay, Sage's memories all concern challenges: keeping the hotel up and running through Hurricane Betsy, working round-the-clock after a fire to turn a three-week closure into just 10 days, even telling LBJ's secret service why he had to be on their floor. "I don't know what your standards are," Sage remembers telling them, "but I have guests other than President Johnson."

Like Gloria Breaux in housekeeping, Larry Johnson in the garage or Joe Bergeron at the belldesk, Sage resists viewing his job as "behind the scenes." Certainly, his lot was to see the hotel not only at its worst but from angles that included behind walls and under sinks. Yet ask him what he spent his life doing and he'll say: taking care of guests.

Sage met guests constantly, he says with pride. Serving them was what his job was all about, serving them day and night, for nearly three decades.

"There was this time," he remembers, "I got called to a guest room on a complaint about the AC." He pauses, then smiles, not wanting to be obscure. "That's the air conditioning. Anyway, this guy tells me all about who he is and what he does and how much he's paying for this room, and he says he and his wife simply won't settle for the way things were. Well, I could tell right away there was nothing wrong with the AC, so there really wasn't anything I could do." Sage stops to think, remembering all it meant to work for the Royal Orleans, to be the Royal Orleans. "So I climbed up there, you know, and banged around on some ductwork. I loosened some things and then tightened them back up, then climbed down the ladder and left.

"You know, everywhere I went for the next few days, I saw this guy and his wife. All they'd tell me is what was great job I'd done, and how everything was just perfect now. See, he thought he wanted help with the AC, but that wasn't what he wanted at all. What he really wanted was service."

A toast to the author from his hotel:
Nassikas with Arthur Hailey.

12

Mr. Hailey's Hotel

There is one more voice that must be heard - one that speaks across the decades with more than the usual style and authority. It is the voice of one who stayed at the Royal Orleans more than once during its early years of operation, and who captured the eternal truths of the hotelman's art in a book that could go by no other name. The voice belongs to Arthur Hailey, and the book, of course, is "Hotel."

A later television series convinced a new generation that "Hotel" was set in San Francisco, where James Brolin, Connie Selleca and others labored to bring the old St. Gregory to life. Yet anyone living in New Orleans can tell you that when Hailey chose to write about hotels, he chose New Orleans to learn all about them. The Royal Orleans became his home away from home - both for his research visits and those conducted by his wife Sheila. In the crush of meeting his publisher's deadline, Hailey even shipped "Hotel" to the Royal Orleans for one last look at its local intelligence.

"The manuscript, as you have it," he wrote to public

relations director Marilyn Barnett in May of 1963, "stops some fifty or sixty pages from the end, which is a hell of a thing to do to anybody, but I'll send you a copy of the full book as soon as it's ready." After marveling at publishing's penchant for rushing past the details, Hailey sent Barnett on her mission. "Specifically, in your reading, I would like you to look for mistakes concerning New Orleans. I want to avoid an Orleanian saying later on, 'If only he'd let someone who lives here look at the manuscript...'"

In the early '60s, as a novelist of some success, Hailey had settled on New Orleans as a special city in which to survey the life of a great hotel. He stayed in several during his succession of visits, vacuuming up piece after piece of information until his St. Gregory combined elements of several. Both the Roosevelt and the St. Charles found their echoes in the inhalings and exhalings of Hailey's hotel. Yet when it came time for Hailey himself to rent a room, most often he chose the Royal Orleans.

Visit after visit, Barnett found herself showing the writer how a hotel operated and which people did what to keep it operating. From introducing him to GM Nassikas to showing him the fine points of Engineering and Housekeeping, the PR director remembers being challenged at every turn by Hailey's questions. As the novel's plot turns at key moments on the activities of the hotel itself, she came to understand slowly the author's concern for accuracy. And she came to respect him all the more.

"Please don't worry about sensitivity," Hailey wrote from home in Ontario. "I'm a professional and, far from being touchy about criticism, am invariably grateful for it. Some of my best ideas have been other people's to begin with. It also helps me to improve my own judgment if people tell me when there is something (a character or scene, or both) which they particularly like."

"Hotel," of course, was a national bestseller, propelling Hailey to the top levels of literary stardom. It became a film starring Rod Taylor and Merle Oberon, and much later, the television series. Yet there remains one scene that all associated with the Royal Orleans did particularly like.

It concerns a French Quarter stroll by protagonist Peter McDermott, the St. Gregory's assistant general manager, and Christine Francis, personal assistant to the establishment's colorful owner. After discussing his career over dinner at Brennan's, Peter takes Christine outside to show her what he hopes his future holds."That's what I'd like to create," he tells her, gazing across Royal Street. "Something at least as good, or maybe better."

As Hailey describes the moment...

"Beneath graceful grilled balconies and fluted iron columns, flickering gas lanterns cast light and shadow on the white-gray classical facade of the Royal Orleans Hotel. Through arched and mullioned windows amber light streamed outward. On the promenade sidewalk a doorman paced, in rich gold uniform and visored pillbox cap. High above, in a sudden breeze, flags and halliards snapped upon their staffs. A taxi drew up. The doorman moved swiftly to open its door. Women's heels clicked and men's laughter echoed as they moved inside. A door slammed. The taxi pulled away.

"'There are some people,' Peter said, 'who believe that the Royal Orleans is the finest hotel in North America. Whether you agree or not doesn't much matter. The point is: It shows how good a hotel can be.'"

Acknowledgements

In Addition to all the people quoted in the text, the author and editors of this volume wish to thank the staff at the Historic New Orleans Collection — who cheerfully answered our many questions and granted permission to reproduce many of these photographs.